The Rise of

ROAD TRANSPORT
1919-1939

CHARLES DUNBAR

LONDON

IAN ALLAN LTD

First published 1981

ISBN 0 7110 1088 9

Published by Ian Allan Ltd, Shepperton, Surrey;
and printed by Ian Allan Printing Ltd at their works
at Coombelands in Runnymede, England

Bibliography

In addition to the government reports referred to in the
text reference has been made to the files of:
Commercial Motor
Modern Transport
Motor Transport (formerly *Motor Traction*)
to *Garcke's Motor Transport Year Book*
and to the statistics published by the British Road
Federation.

The following works have also been consulted:
A Historical Review of McNamara's, 1937
British Lorries, 1900-1945, C. F. Klapper
Commercial Road Vehicles, E. L. Cornwell
Life and Times of Ernest Bevin, Alan Bullock
The Long Haul, Michael Seth-Smith
The Scottish Carter, Angela Tuckett
Transport Saga, 1646-1947 (Pickford's)

Photo Credits

J. Brevitt   62 (both)
C. S. Dunbar   11 (both), 47, 51, 56, 57, 59 (both),
     60 (both), 61, 63, 69(T), 75, 94, 95, 112(T), 139, 140
P. S. Dunbar   10
H. Elliott   34(B)
Ian Allan Library   2, 13(T), 17 (both), 22(B), 24 (both),
     25, 26 (both), 27, 28(T), 29(T), 39(T), 48, 49, 50 (both),
     53, 54 (both), 65, 66, 69(B), 70, 71, 72, 74, 76,
     77 (both), 78, 80, 81, 90 (both), 91, 98 (both), 99,
     101 (both), 102(T), 106, 110, 114, 115, 116 (both), 117,
     118, 119 (both), 127, 130, 131
F. Joseph   15(B), 96, 97, 104 (both), 105 (both), 125
C. F. Klapper   15(T)
Mansell Collection   32, 33, 93 (both), 111
Motor Transport   13(B), 14 (both), 18 (all), 19 (both),
     20, 21 (all), 29(B), 31, 39(B), 40 (both), 41, 42, 43, 44,
     45, 46, 55, 67, 68 (both), 82, 84, 85, 92, 102(B), 103(T),
     112(B), 132, 133, 134, 135, 136
A. Myers   35 (both), 37
National Motor Museum   103(B), 107, 108
Ratcliffe Metals   22(T)
Road Haulage Association   88
Sport & General   28(B)
Temple Pren   138
United Road Transport Workers   87
A. K. C. Ware   34(T)
C. Warwick   113

*Title page: The Associated Equipment Company, well-
established as a builder of buses and heavy lorries, turned to
lighter vehicles in 1924 and produced this 2-tonner with a
24.7hp 4-cylinder petrol engine; although the type was
offered with pneumatic tyres, Cakebread, Robey were
evidently conservative and stuck to solids; they also kept to
oil side-lights.*

Contents

Preface

The twenty years between the two world-wars produced a revolution in inland transport as far-reaching in its economic and social effects as the two decades after 1830, when rail superseded road for all long-distance movement. Exactly the reverse occurred between 1919 and 1939 in the case of goods traffic other than the basic raw materials. Railway shares, which had ranked with government bonds as trustee stock, became almost valueless and great difficulty was experienced in raising sufficient fresh capital to maintain the system. At the same time the reduction in handling, which was often possible by using road transport, and the great flexibility of the motor vehicle contributed greatly to the revival of the late 1930s after the disastrous slump of earlier years. Rearmament, which became urgent after Hitler's accession to power would have been much more difficult had the change not taken place.

Much has been written about vehicle development between 1919 and 1939, but I felt that, to give a complete picture, this needed to be looked at in conjunction with the legal and operating changes which occurred at the same time. As I have been actively connected with road transport in one way or another since 1921 and took a prominent part in the developments of the 1930s, I thought that I would try to tell the story.

I have been able to do this almost entirely from my own records and personal recollections, but have also been glad of assistance on some details. G. W. Quick Smith, who played a prominent part in bringing the trade associations together and went on to great responsibilities after 1945, has been most helpful. John F. Parke, another old friend, has gone out of his way to help and others who have kindly answered my enquiries include Harold Bridges, E. L. Cornwell, P. S. Davies (Bedford Commercial Vehicles), Harold Elliott, Philip Hine, the late C. F. Klapper, Frank Joseph (National Carriers), Jackson Moore (URTU), Arthur Myers, J. T. Rissbrook, Mrs J. Southgate (Chartered Institute of Transport) and Clifford Warwick. Alan Thomas editor of 'Motor Transport', put his great collection of photographs at my disposal and S. W. Stevens-Stratten searched among his for suitable illustrations.

Chapter 1

In 1919 a book was published entitled *The History and Economics of Transport.* It was intended for students taking a commerce degree at Birmingham and other universities. It described how road transport had been replaced, except for short distance movements, by the railways, but it contained not one single word about the internal combustion engine. The authors were not alone in failing to recognise the revolution in transport that had already begun. The government of the day, in reorganising the main line railways into four groups by the Railways Act, 1921, sought, by a new classification of freight charges, to guarantee them net returns running at the same rate as the profits of the companies before 1914. No one, apparently, realised that the traditional method of charging ('what the traffic will bear') was going to play right into the hands of a rapidly developing rival, so that the railways never again enjoyed their pre-1914 profitability.

Even if the text book mentioned above was written before 1919 and publication had been held up by the war, one would have thought that the authors would have seen the signs of the coming change. The government certainly should have done so by 1921.

It was not as though motor transport suddenly burst on the scene in 1919. The development of steam on the railways was accompanied by experiments on the highways, but poor surface conditions and legal prohibitions on speed combined to hinder the development of mechanical traction on the roads, so that, in practice, most steam-driven vehicles were confined to the drawing of heavy loads, usually within a small radius. The traction engine pulling a load-carrying trailer was a familiar sight, but rarely seen outside the main centres of population. The furthest regular runs by steamers were probably in connection with the textile trades of Lancashire and Yorkshire where steam-propelled lorries played an important part in carrying raw materials from the ports to the mills and finished goods from the mills to the ports. They continued to do so into the fourth decade of the century and when the East Lancashire road from Walton to Irlams o'th' Height was built in 1928-9, hydrants were located at the side of it every few miles from which water could be obtained through a slot meter.

By 1914 the petrol engine had come to be regarded as a logical and reliable propulsion unit for local passenger transport in London, but it was very little used outside the metropolitan area. Elsewhere generally speaking, the electric tram was unchallenged as a mass carrier. There were some small exceptions: Eastbourne, which started motor buses in 1903, and Widnes, which began services in 1906, never had trams.

As early as 1885, the Germans Gottlieb Daimler and Karl Benz, proved the practicability of petrol-driven vehicles but the idea was slow to catch on. Teething troubles were prolonged and, in some instances, firms bold enough to introduce motor vans or lorries found themselves in serious financial trouble. Such a one was McNamara & Company, carriers of the Royal Mail from 1837, which in 1905 put into service two 7cwt vans on German chassis for work in the City. These were followed by Dennis and Leyland vehicles, so that by 1913, McNamara had 67 motors, mostly on Post Office work. In 1906 a regular service was started between London and Slough and in 1908 night mails were put on from London to Southampton and London to Portsmouth. In August 1911 a night service to Bristol was started, using a 30cwt Dennis chassis with a maximum load of 18cwt. In these years too, nightly journeys were started between Worthing, Brighton and London for market produce and other goods. In 1907, McNamara obtained a contract to supply two 30cwt vans to the wholesale druggists, Maw, Son & Sons, and soon after similar contracts were arranged with two other wholesale druggists. Unfortunately, McNamara's return on the capital invested in motor traction was insufficient and in 1913 the company was put into receivership, pending eventual reconstruction in 1921.

Pickfords was the most famous of the pre-1914 carriers, with a history going back to the 17th century, but it was more cautious than McNamara in introducing internal combustion machines. Its first motor, a 2-cylinder James and Brown chassis, which was fitted with a body for carrying linen between St Bartholomew's Hospital and a laundry at Swanley, gave much trouble, but the company had better luck with two Commer Cars, also bought in 1907 and used on inter-depot work. The 5ton Commers, which

Above: *This 30-cwt parcels van, shown restored, is included as typical of the small carriers who, well into the 1930s, worked into the large towns and continued to use solid tyred vans to a late date; Yeomans worked into Birmingham from Four Oaks, nine miles out, and used this until 1934; the engine (40hp) and chassis were built by the Continental Engine Co of Detroit, the gearbox came from the Fuller Gear Co of Kalamazoo and the electrical equipment was by the Northern Electric Co of New York; the vehicle, which was built in 1916, was left behind by the Americans; it was rebodied by Henry Garner of Birmingham and registered in 1920.*

followed, were advanced vehicles for their day as they had pre-selector gears, but when 1914 came Pickford's mechanical traction was predominantly steam-driven.

Carter, Paterson, the London parcel carrier with which Pickfords had a working agreement from 1912, bought a Daimler van in 1896, but it was destroyed in a stable fire and it was not until about 1911 that the company seriously began to use motors in place of horses.

The development of heavy commercial chassis made little progress before 1914 and the great majority of motor vans and lorries then on the road were light vehicles, often on private car chassis. Their use was limited to parcels work, but it was ancillary users, rather than the professional carriers, who were most attracted to them. Harrods, the great London departmental store, bought a Dennis van in 1904, although most of the delivery vehicles it purchased during the next 10 years were driven by electric batteries. The Barnsley British Co-operative Society bought motor vans from 1899 onwards but relied on steam well into the 1920s for heavy loads. Prominent before 1910 in the service of the departmental stores in the West End of London was the name of Lacre (made up from Long Acre, the thoroughfare where the business started), now only associated with vehicles supplied to municipal cleansing departments.

Among provincial carriers running more than local journeys with mechanically-propelled vehicles before World War I were B. E. Barrett of Luton; W. T. Burrows & Son of Maidstone, who started a service to London in June 1914; H. Viney & Co Ltd of Preston

10

whose steamers were a familiar sight in Lancashire and Yorkshire; H. Hamp & Sons of Northampton; O. & C. Holdsworth of Halifax; John Bennett Ltd of Leith with a service to Glasgow from April 1911; Arthur Murray of Bury, running to other South Lancashire towns from 1909; Smithers & Sons of Wimbledon and Kingston, who started in 1910; Taylors Garage of Falmouth (March 1914); A. Walters & Sons of Hitchin, operating to London from May 1914; Wiggs & Sons Ltd of Peckham (1912); William Harper & Sons of Liverpool operating steamers from 1908; C. & G. Yeoman of Canterbury (1906).

The way in which mixed fleets were used can be illustrated by a description of how Peek Frean's biscuits were delivered within a 30-mile radius of London. According to *Motor Traction* of 1 January 1919, the firm had been able to carry on during the war with three Aveling & Porter 5ton steamers, two Edison 1ton battery-electrics, one Tilling-Stevens 4ton petrol-electric, one Tilling-Stevens 1ton, six Dennis 30cwt, one Straker-Squire 5ton and one 1ton, one Albion 1ton and of course, horses.

Above: *Although this vehicle was earlier than 1919, the picture is of great historical interest; it is the 5ton tractor which won the War Office trials in 1901.*

Below: *Thomas Clarkson of Chelmsford had considerable success with his steam buses, especially after changing from coke to paraffin for the fuel, but his lorries did not take on; only one is known to have been registered as a coke-burner, but it is said that 20 chassis, originally built with bus bodies, were converted for use as lorries.*

Chapter 2

When the new century began there were some professional soldiers in France and Germany who foresaw that motor transport might play an important part in war time, but the idea was not seriously considered in Britain by the pundits of the General Staff. Looking back, the use of cavalry in World War 1 now seems an almost incredible anachronism, but with the mentality of the time at the War Office, it was surprising that motors were used at all. Rather reluctantly, some trials of mechanical vehicles were organised in 1901 and in 1908 a subsidy scheme was started, at first only available for steam traction-engines. Operators who were willing to buy vehicles which the War Office thought might be useful were given a grant on the understanding that the vehicles could be taken over if and when war broke out. In 1911 the scheme was extended to motor vehicles, divided into two classes — 'A' for 3-ton loads and 'B' for 30cwt. The small starting subsidy of £8 or £12 was raised in 1914 to £120 payable in four instalments over three years.

Unfortunately, the military authorities, with little or no practical experience, attempted to lay down uniform specifications for the subsidy vehicles, which, in practice, produced many faults when they were mobilised in 1914. Manufacturers then on the subsidy list were Albion, Dennis, Hallford, Karrier, Leyland, Maudslay, Thornycroft (famous for its J type) and Wolseley.

Surprising omissions from the list were the Associated Equipment Co of Walthamstow, builder of the famous London B type bus, Lacre (already mentioned), Commer Cars of Luton and D. Napier & Son Ltd. Lacre products gave particularly good service to the Belgian Army, but after the war the company concentrated on mechanical road-sweepers.

At the end of the war, the Army owned 66,352 lorries, scattered all over the world. Of these 6,411 were Leylands including the heavy-duty type which became known as RAF after it became standard in the Air Force. When it was announced that the government intended to sell the bulk of its vast fleet by auction, the Leyland company realised that such a flood would kill the market for new vehicles. With this in mind, coupled with a desire to preserve its name for reliability, Leyland bought back 3,111 lorries and took

over an aeroplane hangar at Ham, near Kingston, Surrey, to recondition them before sale. Dennis, the first maker to persevere with the now universal worm drive, provided about 7,000 trucks to the forces during the war but figured relatively little in post-war sales to hauliers. Instead the firm concentrated with success on fire-engines and bus chassis.

Of the B type buses running in London in 1914, 1,319 were requisitioned for service in France and their reliability prompted the War Office to ask AEC to supply chassis to conform to subsidy specifications. The result was the steel-framed Y type of which over 10,000 were made. Like Leyland, AEC bought back many of its vehicles at the end of the war and reconditioned them before sale, while at the same time launching a programme of new construction. Both Commer and Napier were also called on to supply lorries for the Army.

Many American vehicles were left in Europe, as not being worth the cost of shipping back, so that for some years after the war, such makes as Mack, FWD, Peerless and Pierce-Arrow were to be seen on British roads. Pierce-Arrow had actually made substantial sales to commercial users in this country during the war when British chassis were unobtainable and this despite the very high price, for those days, of £1,805 for a 5ton truck. FWD incorporated an English

Above right: Thornycroft was in the motor business from the beginning and its J type lorry became famous during World War 1; many were sold for civilian use after the war and this may be one of them, as the Crow Carrying Co Ltd bought it in May 1920; although Crow handled some general merchandise it was as a carrier of fuel and other liquids that it became prominent; in 1920 bulk tankers were unknown and this high-sided lorry was intended to carry 1,000gal of fuel in 2gal tins.

Right: Lacre is a name that for 50 years has been associated with the adaption of chassis for road-sweepers and dust-carts, but the firm started as chassis manufacturers themselves in Long Acre, London (hence the name); this 1925 product was already out of date then; notice the solid tyres (on a 2ton van!) and the chain-drive; the only advanced feature was the one-piece side-panels in 12-gauge aluminium.

Above: *A very rare bird was the Watson, a make which had disappeared by 1930; made in Newcastle the chassis with a 4-cylinder engine had an unusual final drive; the road wheels carried epicyclic gear rings on their inner faces which engaged with pinions carried on the half-shaft ends of a conventional drive axle.*

Below: *Napier was noticeable in World War 1 for the high-speed cars it provided for the top brass; it also made a few commercial chassis before becoming world-famous for its aero engines; nothing is known about the two 2-tonners in the picture, but they may have been government surplus; Duncan used them for carrying fish from Liverpool docks.*

company in 1921 — Four Wheel Drive Motors Ltd based at Slough — but this faded out in the 1930s. The famous Slough dump was also the base for Slough Lorries and Components Ltd which was used as the Peerless trading company in Britain. A reconditioned Peerless 5 tonner could be bought in 1919 for £255.

Towards the end of the war 250 acres at Kempton Racecourse were used as a receiving centre for all new vehicles prior to their distribution to the forces.

Production did not stop automatically when the armistice came at 11am on 11 November 1918 and for months after the end of hostilities vehicles continued to arrive at Kempton Park, until at last questions were asked in Parliament about the thousands of vehicles lying there unused. What was originally referred to as the Cippenham Repair Depot also contained many hundreds of vehicles and it was this that came to be called the Slough dump.

Right: Although this photo was actually taken in 1908, the railways continued to use pair-horse lorries like this well into the 1920s; accidents to van boys were frequent — not surprisingly in view of their precarious perch.

Below: The railways continued to use steamers well into the 1920s.

Chapter 3

In the first flush of post-war expansion, chassis were used indiscriminately for goods and passenger work. It was quite common for a lorry to be used for general haulage from Monday to midday Saturday and then have its body lifted off and replaced by something more suitable for carrying passengers, but, before long, separate chassis began to be developed for the two different functions and eventually most manufacturers concentrated the bulk of their production (in some cases, all of it) on either one or the other. The General Strike of 1926 can be taken as the event which, more than anything else, brought about the permanent division between passenger and goods operation. The practice of using what were essentially car chassis for small vans gradually died out during the 1920s.

The biggest technical change in this decade was perhaps, the general abandonment of chain-drive except for the heaviest vehicles. Scammell was still making chain-driven lorries into the 1930s but it was alone. Even Albion, whose 3ton chain-driven subsidy type was famous, changed over to worm-drive. Scammell became well known for its development of articulation. In 1921 it brought out a 4-wheel tractor to be used with a 2-wheel trailer, so that 10ton could be carried without exceeding the then legal axle weights, but the idea of articulation made only slow progress. The drawbar trailer was more popular for long-distance work and had operational advantages as the trailer could be left at one delivery or collection point while the towing vehicle was engaged elsewhere. Another Scammell winner in this decade was the frameless tanker. When its practicability was proved, it led to major changes in the handling of liquids and, although these were not fully effective until after World War II, the first experiments with the bulk handling of milk took place in the 1920s.

An alternative to the articulated vehicle which became increasingly popular for both goods and passenger work late in this decade was the multi-wheeler rigid chassis; this was used not only for petrol driven vehicles but also for steamers, Foden for example, Guy, GMC and Maudslay were prominent in this development and the Leyland Hippo was on the market before the decade ended.

One would naturally expect the 6-wheeler to be confined to heavy loads, but, rather amusingly, a Trojan came out in 1929 with six wheels to carry only 15cwt. The Trojan was a strange little beast, intended for local deliveries, which a surprised public first saw in 1924. Built by (of all people) Leyland, it had thin solid tyres and a 10hp 2-stroke engine.

Leyland, presumably, wanted to break into the small van market, where specially built bodies on car chassis were common well into the decade. This was the case with Dodge, which sent over American-built chassis and constructed suitable bodies to order here, before producing commercial chassis about 1930. In the immediate post-war years many other American lightweight vehicles were available. Chevrolet, Reo and of course, Ford are names that spring to mind. Ford vans had been assembled at Trafford Park from 1916 and there was almost an industry in the 1920s fitting extensions to Ford chassis so that greater loads could be carried. General Motors, not having had much success with imported Chevrolets, eventually acquired control of Vauxhall Motors and in 1931 began production of Bedfords at Luton.

Reference has already been made to early Commer models with the epicyclic gearboxes and to Commer Cars' contribution to the war. In the post-war years the company was unable to obtain sufficient orders to keep it solvent and in 1926 it became a subsidiary of Humber, the car manufacturer, and so two years later, passed into the Rootes Group. It then went ahead with considerable success in both the light and medium heavy ranges.

But it is to Morris that the credit must go for starting mass production of light commercial vehicles, which under the name of Morris-Commercial made at

Above right: *The first Scammell 6-wheel frameless fuel oil tanker built in 1923, with a capacity of 2,000gal was powered by a 4-cylinder petrol engine driving through a 3-speed box and an intermediate jackshaft with final chain drive; sprockets on the jackshaft could be changed to vary the gear ratios; the driver had little protection with only a canvas hood.*

Right: *Horse-traction took a long time to die out and, in its last years, the lot of the horses was eased in many cases by the use of pneumatic tyres.*

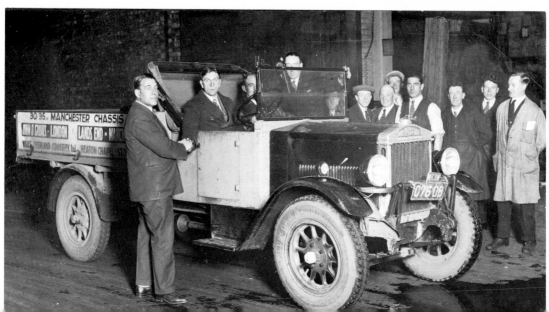

Top left: *The 4 ton Dennis of 1925, a typical middle-weight of the period, with 4-cylinder petrol engine and crash gearbox, but, a little unusual, the Dennis worm-drive to the rear axle; oil lamps were still carried, but is that an acetylene headlamp on the nearside front dumbiron?*

Centre left: *Don't assume that ox-wagons were a common form of transport on the Portsmouth road in the 1920s; the Albion was more typical of the times.*

Left: *The solemn expressions suggest at first sight that the intrepid driver of this truck is off on a dare-devil expedition to the end of the earth; in fact he was about to drive a Manchester from the factory at Stockport to John O'Groats then to Land's End on to London and back to Stockport — 1,913 miles which he covered in 63hr 45min running time — and there were no motorways then; the Manchester was an American style commercial chassis assembled by Willys-Overland Crossley.*

Top: *One of the most curious vehicles ever produced in quantity was the little Trojan — a Leyland product too! It had a 10hp 4-cylinder 2-stroke petrol engine, a pedal operated epicyclic gearbox and thin solid tyres; this model supplied to the GPO in 1925 had pressed-steel wheels with imitation spokes.*

Above: *A Ford was common place, of course, in the 1920s but Renault vans, with their coal-scuttle bonnets and radiators behind them, were more unusual; at the time this picture was taken in 1925 the author had some in his fleet of newspaper vans with magneto ignition and, presumably these were the same; 'Amplion' was the trade name of a wireless manufacturer.*

19

Adderley Park, Birmingham scooped a large part of the market from 1924 onwards. Today Morris and Austin are almost automatically associated together, but at this period they were, of course, fiercely in competition but it was competition which from 1925 onwards was restricted to private cars, as at that time Austin gave up making commercial vehicles.

Pickfords, among the strongest supporters of steam haulage for heavy loads over long distances, was led to make a change by the performance of a Saurer coach it bought for a Swiss tour, when, for a short time, it engaged in passenger work. It ordered 50 5ton lorries with 5ton trailers from Saurer and eventually bought 110. Its chief engineer (later general manager), W. J. Elliott, emphasised the importance of this move by sending his son, Harold (later himself general manager) to train at the Saurer works.

But the steamer was not by any means dead. Clayton, Foden, Fowler, Garrett, Sentinel and Yorkshire all sold well during the 1920s, and refinements were continually being made to reduce the amount of physical effort required to increase the range of operation and improve the manoeuvrability of the steamer. It was legislation in the next decade that killed this typically British method of transport.

With the exception of the Trojan, all lightweight

Above: Historians will probably be more familiar with the name of Straker-Squire as maker of motor bus chassis, but it also built private cars, steam wagons, trolley buses and haulage vehicles; after several reconstructions the company launched a new programme in 1925, including the A type, used for this 5-tonner; it was described as having a single plate disc clutch; leaf springs in place of valve rocker arms and ball and socket shackles for the suspension springs; 'the new programme' was Straker-Squire's last effort to stay in business.

vehicles in the 1920s were normally supplied with pneumatic tyres, but even at the end of the decade many of the heaviest lorries were still on solids. Pickfords made a significant change in 1924 when vans on pneumatic tyres began to replace solid tyred steamers.

Compression-ignition engines of German make made their appearance here in 1928, but were not widely adopted until the mid-1930s.

By 1930, most drivers of commercial vehicles at least had windscreens. The use of timber declined and metal and composite bodies appeared, a tendency which the Road Traffic Act, 1930, hastened by fixing the low upper-weight limit of $2\frac{1}{2}$ton for a 30mph vehicle.

Right: *Bean Cars was a Tipton, Staffs firm, which made both private cars and commercial vehicles and had some success in overseas sales; it was killed by the depression of the early 1930s, but the factory still remains, making parts for some of the Leyland products.*

Centre: *One of the great names in transport before nationalisation was McNamara, going back to 1837; besides operating extensive services itself it had a big business in contract vehicles, notably for the GPO; Evans, Sons Lescher and Webb were also prominent hirers; this is one of the popular types of the day, a Dennis 30cwt; an amusing point is that the spare wheel was not on a pneumatic but on a cushion-tyre!*

Below: *A demonstration Super-Sentinel of 1928, pressing the point that the mining industry was in a bad way; a 6-wheel version could carry 14tons at a fuel cost, it was claimed, of less than 2d per mile.*

Above: *When J. F. Ratcliffe wanted to give his staff a day out in 1921, he let them have the firm's T-model Ford; history doesn't record how far they went, but they must have had a blustery time!*

Below: *Like G. A. Renwick, E. W. Rudd was also on the board of Scammell lorries; this rigid example, built in 1930, shows the chain-drive, with which Scammell persisted to a relatively late date.*

Chapter 4

The decade after World War I ended has been described as 'the roaring twenties' and it was certainly the era of young men rushing into transport, working without thought of time and travelling regardless of distance. To take only one example of thousands, there was young Joe Male of Pensnett in the Black Country, gassed in the war and wanting an open-air life, going to a dump in South Wales in 1919, buying an ex WD Peerless 2-tonner and getting it back to Pensnett somehow, although he had never driven before. Thus he founded a business which still exists.

A more spectacular performance was that of Roger W. Sewill, who, with Guy S. Moser and Gertrude M. Sewill, launched London & Southern Counties Transport Co Ltd on 12 November 1919 and began operations from a depot in Gas House Road, Reigate. After a fairly normal development, gradually expanding westward, Sewill astonished everyone with his Flowers Express, which, left Penzance or Newlyn with flowers from the Scillies and delivered them in London, 280 miles or more away, in 20 hours, despite the legal speed limit of 20mph. Sewill's vans all carried the legend 'Spans the South' and his company was generally known in the trade as 'Spans'. The Flowers Express vans were frequently trapped by the police and the company was heavily fined for speeding.

R. W. Angell, after war service, went into business at Bognor as a coal merchant and soon added haulage. He discovered scope for transport from London of small lots of groceries to the seaside towns of West Sussex and, by 1928, when Carter, Paterson took an interest in the business, had built up a parcels network extending over much of Hampshire and Sussex. A depot was built on a disused RAF base at Yapton and in 1931 a nightly service between there and Birmingham was started.

Harold Bridges of Preston left school at 13 and after a great struggle managed to raise £250 to buy a model T Ford in 1921, leaving himself with £1 working capital. The parcels business he slowly built up was nationalised in 1950 for £128,000. In 1951 he was able to start up again and eventually sold this second business in 1966 to Tayforth, a subsidiary of the British Transport Commission, for £1,350,000. But this is looking a long way ahead and Bridges' success cannot be regarded as typical. Many thousands got no further than their first lorry and that was often repossessed by the finance companies.

Those who came in after the first mad rush was over often did better. Clifford Warwick of Birmingham, after discharge from the RAF, set up a greengrocery round with a horse and cart and by 1923 felt safe in risking £132 in buying a 1ton Ford. He went to market at 4.30am and, when his round was done, found other work for the lorry. Before long he had launched into general haulage using 4-and 5-tonners. Using his market experience, he started a service to Birmingham for the market gardeners in the Vale of Evesham. Services from Wisbech and to and from London followed and then came work from manufacturing firms in Birmingham, so that, by 1939, he had 27 vehicles, including some low loaders.

Frank McKeen was a fitter at the Christchurch gasworks when one evening in January 1923, he saw in *The Bournemouth Daily Echo* an advertisement for someone with a large motorcycle combination to undertake delivery work for the paper. I had joined the *'Echo'* in October 1922 as circulation manager and started pushing the paper out into the country using hired vehicles to test possibilities. McKeen had a Harley-Davidson and he was engaged to work a round each evening up the Avon Valley. About this time he heard that a chain of chemists shops in Bournemouth were sending photographic negatives to Southampton for development and printing. Having offered these people a daily service, McKeen took the bold step of giving up his regular job and canvassing for other business between Bournemouth and Southampton. Before long he had sufficient work to buy a 2ton van. He then gave up the *'Echo'* round and concentrated on general carrying, his biggest customer being a Pokesdown manufacturer of rock, whose products he delivered over a large area of southern England. Eventually Mac Carriers Ltd was formed and opened a London depot in Union Road, Clapham. In the early 1930s it acquired control of Roberts of Norwich and in December 1932 both businesses were sold to the Bouts-Tillotson group. 'Mac' and his wife then went into the entertainment world as owners of the Boscombe Hippodrome and a cinema at Winton.

Two other haulage businesses developed from the hire of combinations to *The Bournemouth Daily Echo*

Above left: *The Wynn family have been prominent hauliers in South Wales for generations; they lost their general haulage business on nationalisation, but have become widely-known as specialists in the movement of abnormal loads; this Scammell 12ton rigid six was a trunk vehicle in the old days.*

Left: *Pickfords' reply to the MRS claim to have the largest lorry in the world; also capable of carrying 100ton on its swan-neck trailer drawn by a Scammell tractor, it is here seen carrying a 90ton transformer from Hollingwood to the Barton Power Station, near Trafford Park, on 23 February 1937.*

Above: *The Marston brothers were prominent in the industry in the 1930s and early specialised in the handling of abnormal indivisible loads; they were particularly proud of their 100-tonner, evolved in conjunction with Scammell and the first able to carry such weights; in this picture, taken in April 1930, the steering wheel for the rear-bogies can be seen and also the motor-cycle used by crew members to go ahead and check the route.*

in my time. L. Jacobs and W. Lavers both started in this way. Jacobs, after several years of independence, sold out to South Coast Carriers and became its Bournemouth manager, but Lavers remained on his own in a small way until he retired in 1958.

Arthur Myers of Bradford, who had been trained as an engineer in the textile industry, discovered in the course of travelling about repairing machinery, that there was no road service for small lots of textiles between Yorkshire and Leicestershire, so on 9 December 1929, in partnership with Norman Gregson (who died in 1933), he started The Bradford-Leicester Parcel Express (later called Bradford-Leicester Transport Ltd), with a central depot at Meadowhead, Sheffield. In 1935, he agreed to go in with the Hanson & Holdsworth group, which will be referred to later. BLT's trunk services during the 1930s were from Bradford and Sheffield to Birmingham and to Kettering and Wellingborough.

The older firms were not idle during this period. Outside London, Pickfords in effect, went out of the parcel carrying business in the 1920s, but its departments handling household removals, meat and heavy machinery expanded considerably. The meat carrying section grew as the result of Pickfords being acquired by Hay's Wharf Cartage Company in 1920.

When Hay's Wharf Cartage came into railway ownership in 1933, Pickfords' interest in parcels revived. A new large depot to handle the London

traffic was opened on railway land at Willow Walk, Bermondsey, in 1935 and another, also on railway land, at Walter Street, Nechells, Birmingham. Both were rail connected. In 1936 Pickfords gained control of three old-established businesses which were operating cargo boats between the Hampshire ports and the Isle of Wight. These were Chaplins Ltd, Crouchers Ltd and Shepherd Bros Ltd. The acquisition of Chaplins was particularly interesting. The original Chaplin was a carrier, who with considerable foresight, threw in his lot with the London & South Western Railway at the start and Chaplins became cartage contractors to the new line.

Left and below left: There was a great deal of competition for abnormal loads between Edward Box and Norman E. Box; the old-style traction engine was used well into the 1930s for heavy loads, despite the low speed limits of 3mph in towns and 5mph elsewhere; the Edward Box vehicle is carrying a diesel-electric locomotive and the Norman E. Box outfit is working for Vickers-Armstrong of Barrow.

Below: What is the man doing with his shoulder against the girder; is he worried in case the trailer swings into the lamppost?; it is not clear from this picture how the rear bogie was steered; the motive-power is thought to be a Scammell; the London & North Eastern Railway had the job of taking this stator from Newcastle to Brighton in August 1933.

Carter, Paterson, as motors replaced horses, closed many of its inner London depots and built new ones in the suburbs, with its central London work concentrated at Macclesfield Road. Although mainly a London business, it had, before 1914, started motor runs to Brighton, Hastings, Margate, Southend and places in the Home Counties where it had agents. In the 1920s it began to buy provincial carriers, starting with R. W. Angell's South Coast Carriers, in which it first took an interest in 1928 and obtained control in 1931. In 1932 Carter, Paterson formed Leicester & County Carriers Ltd which took over a business which had started in 1924 as a clearing house. Finally, in 1933, it bought Karriers Parcels Delivery Service, started in Liverpool by W. S. Finlayson in 1919.

McNamara's long distance goods services had to be suspended during World War I, but the firm quickly decided on a policy of buying businesses which had sprung up in Birmingham, Bradford, Bristol, Leicester and Liverpool and starting trunk services linking them with London and with each other, so giving a reliable nightly service for parcels. The Bradford base was, apparently, given up at an early date, but the services between the other centres continued without a break (except during the General Strike of 1926) until World War II made changes necessary.

The old family firm of Sutton & Co which had built up its business by using the railways for inter-depot work, began its own trunk services with a nightly run between London and Birmingham on 21 August 1921.

Above left and left: *Only through road transport was it possible to maintain essential supplies during the General Strike of 1926; the Government hired lorries wherever it could and provided military escorts, as in this picture of meat arriving at Smithfield; the RAF convoy is passing the Mansion House.*

Above: *In the early 1920s petrol pumps began to appear at garages, so necessitating the bulk transport of fuel; Crow bought this AEC with semi-trailer in 1926, by which time it had moved from South Woodford to Barking.*

Right: *Roger W. Sewill, always associated in the early days with 'Spans the South', ceased to be an executive director of London & Southern Counties Transport in 1935 on appointment as national director of Associated Road Operators.*

Atlas Express, also of mid-Victorian origin, started using motors for collection and delivery work in 1919, but continued to use the railways for sending parcels between depots until after World War II. Sandersons, an old parcels carrier in the Midlands also continued to rely on rail connections and seems to have faded out in the 1930s without ever starting any trunk services by road.

London was a magnet which increasingly attracted provincial hauliers during this period, not only for general haulage but notably for specialised work. Country carriers of Northamptonshire and Leicestershire, who had been content to work in and out of the numerous small towns in those counties, replaced their horses by motors and began experimental journeys to London with 'loose' boots, ie boots in one-pair cartons instead of in large cartons or crates containing a number of pairs. The saving in packing and the speedier and more direct delivery thus offered appealed so greatly to manufacturers that by 1930 every town in the two counties was connected directly to London, with hosiery as well being carried. What could be done in one direction could be done in others and so a web of services spread out from the East Midlands to all the major centres in the provinces.

Another specialist traffic was the carriage of straw hats from Luton, particularly interesting because to accommodate these light but bulky articles vans were built with an extension over the driver's cab, a feature which itself became known as the 'Luton'.

The increasing use of internal combustion engines brought specialisation in the field of petrol distribution. Crow Carrying Co Ltd of Barking was registered in June 1920 and, from the start concentrated on this work. The old firm of H. Viney & Co of Preston started a separate company, Lancashire Petrol Deliveries, in 1926 and this expanded to include the carriage of industrial alcohols, benzol and coal-tar products.

The reliability of small, fast vans on pneumatic tyres was quickly appreciated by film renters. The cinema industry was booming and the twice-weekly change of films round each circuit called for smart schedules. Several firms sprang up specialising in this work, of which the most prominent was the business finally known as FTS (Great Britain) Ltd.

At the other extreme from parcel carrying is the carriage of abnormal indivisible loads. Steam traction engines were widely used for this purpose before 1914 and this was the section of the industry in which the change to internal combustion engines was slowest. As late as 1926, the best-known firm in this work, Norman E. Box of Manchester, was relying on steel-wheeled Fowler road locomotives, of which it had 15. These were able to draw a great variety of trailers,

including some low-loaders only a foot off the ground. The use of rubber tyres, even solid ones, was only just beginning for this work, but in 1927 Pickfords, which had had an important heavy haulage department before the war, also relying on steam, put on the road an articulated low-loader on rubber tyres. When Box brought out a 100-tonner, Pickfords replied with a trailer having 32 wheels and 64 solid tyres and capable of carrying 160 tons.

Pickfords had started using motor vans for market work in 1912 but, until well after World War 1, most market work (not only the carriage of meat but also of fruit and vegetables) was done by horses, which often had the advantage of being more easily backed into narrow spaces and against awkwardly-placed loading decks than motor vehicles. The 1920s saw a movement away from rail for the long-distance conveyance of meat and, inspired perhaps by Roger Sewill's activities, Pickfords in 1932 ordered a special AEC to carry 110 sides of beef at a constant temperature between Aberdeen and London. The economics of this operation would make interesting reading but they have never been made public.

Pickfords made all its own bodies. This was also the case, on a smaller scale, with Market Transport Ltd of Balham, started in 1921 by two brothers, P. J. R. and E. T. J. Tapp. In the course of years, this came to concentrate almost entirely on the retail distribution of meat from Smithfield and of other foodstuffs from manufacturers in the Home and Southern Counties. Eventually Market Transport not only built most of its own bodies but the Tapps set up a separate bodybuilding business, County Commercial Cars Ltd at Fleet, Hants.

T. M. Fairclough & Sons Ltd was another family business concerned with the meat trade which motorised in the 1920s. In the fruit and vegetable markets Geo Monro Ltd was a wellknown carrier and Mr G. Monro himself was a prominent member of the Commercial Motor Users Association.

An important development was the start in 1928 of a service for smalls between Yorkshire and London, jointly operated by Joseph Hanson & Son of Huddersfield (with an ancestry as old as Pickfords) and I. W. Holdsworth & Co of Halifax, a business that was certainly engaged in carrying in the 1860s. Both concerns had been closely connected with the textile trades and, from local beginnings, had developed cross-Pennine services before starting the London venture.

They both became concerned with passenger transport as well and Hanson's Buses survived as an independent until in 1969 it was absorbed into the Huddersfield Corporation undertaking. Holdsworth started a bus business in 1921 which became part of West Yorkshire Road Car Co and in 1924 formed

Above: *London & Southern Counties Transport it may have been officially, but to every road user in southern England it was 'Spans'; its runs with flowers from Cornwall became an epic, but it also handled general foods and, at one time, meat, as well as collecting milk churns from farms; when this picture of the Reigate depot was taken in 1928, the fleet consisted of nine Leylands (two of which are shown here), two Albions and two Fords.*

another, Hebble Motor Services, which it later sold to the British Electric Traction group. The start of the London service was followed by other long-distance ventures and a number of acquisitions, the story of which comes in the next decade.

The great majority of the long-distance services in and out of London, which came into being in the 1920s originated from the provinces, but the Bouts brothers of East London, beginning in 1922, started services to Manchester and to Leeds. Their vehicles, large box vans painted white, were very distinctive and one long 6-wheeler was well known to habitual users of A45 as 'the showboat'.

Some large fleets were built up by industrial groups. Bristol Industries Ltd, a Wills family business with interests over a wide field of manufacture, started Bristol Haulage Co in 1919 and began trunking to and from London. In the next decade it took control of several other transport firms.

J. Coventon Moth started Coventons Ltd of Holloway before 1914 and this company seems to have been absorbed eventually into Metropolitan Transport Supply, a wholly-owned subsidiary of Kearley & Tonge, the wholesale grocers. Moth was involved with Scammell and A. G. Scammell was on the board of Coventons. Moth was also concerned with the start of Commer Cars.

Northern Motor Utilities of York, while not a Rowntree subsidiary, was closely associated with that firm from its start in 1919. China Clays of St Austell started Heavy Transport Co Ltd in 1920 and it still exists as a wholly-owned subsidiary. Talbot-Serpell Transport Co Ltd of Reading became identified with the carriage of biscuits.

Other familiar names in the 1920s were Allied Transport Ltd of White City, Birmingham (A. P. Watson, W. B. Dronsfield and E. L. Watson), Barnsley Transport Co Ltd (which seems to have had a family connection with the West Riding Automobile Co), Boston Transport Co Ltd, Brighton & South Coast Haulage Ltd, C. C. Morton & Co Ltd of Liverpool and Manchester, London & South Coast Transport Ltd (from 1922 Cambrian Coaching & Goods Transport Ltd), Charles Poulter Ltd of London, E. Child & Pullin Ltd of Ipswich, City & Suburban Carriers Ltd (originally a collection and delivery agent for Herd, Barter & Gerner, shipping

Left and above: *Covent Garden and Billingsgate, showing, like the Borough Market, a glorious mixture of motors, horse-carts and barrows; the railway vehicles would be bringing supplies in from the main line stations; note the salesmen in dustcoats and bowlers and the porters (bottom right) wearing hard-crowned hats on which fish-boxes could be carried.*

Above: *Both horse-power and man power were prominent in the London market areas in the 1920s and 1930s; this picture (actually taken after the outbreak of war) is typical; the old Hop Exchange (by then not used for that purpose) is where the signs hang out and the carts and lorries are waiting for produce from the Borough Market.*

Left: *W. J. ('Big Bill') Elliott, general manager of Pickfords, at the opening of the new Willow Walk, Bermondsey parcels depot in 1935, which was to have been managed by Harry Flegg; because of Flegg's illness Harold Elliott took on the job.*

Above right and right: *Two views of the Bradford-Leicester Transport Cos depot at Sheffield in 1938; note the different method of deck construction compared with the Red Arrow example on page 59.*

agents: later absorbed into Carter, Paterson), Currie & Co (Newcastle) Ltd, Downer & Co Ltd of London and Southampton, Durtnalls Ltd of Brighton, George Park Ltd of Portsmouth, Glasgow Hiring Co Ltd, J. Blake & Co Ltd of Liverpool, Kinder's Garage & Haulage Ltd of Blaby, Leicester, Kneller & Chandler Ltd (London-Birmingham service), Lep Transport & Depository Ltd, (then working from Castle Street, Long Acre, London), Marshall Bros (Carriers) Ltd of Leeds, Motor Carriers (Liverpool) Ltd, E. W. Rudd Ltd of Bow, Henry Russett & Sons of Bristol, Ryburn Garage & Transport Co Ltd of Sowerby Bridge, Stott's Motors Ltd of Oldham, Sutherland Trading Co Ltd, Southern Roadways Ltd of Poole, Southern Transport Co Ltd of Brighton, Thomas Allen Ltd of Wapping (soon to become a subsidiary of Coast Lines Ltd), Topham Bros (Manchester) Ltd, W. E. Chivers & Sons Ltd of Devizes, C. & G. Yeoman of Canterbury, already mentioned.

The main line railways had no general road powers until 1928 and in many areas used local cartage firms for collection and delivery. In some cases this association went back to the earliest days of the railways. In Glasgow there was Wordie & Co Ltd established in 1700 and in Edinburgh Mutter, Howey & Co Ltd. The Great Western Railway employed George & Matthews Ltd of Wolverhampton which was also in business as 'canal steerers'. These firms were slow to mechanise because, as in the case of the market work, already mentioned, the horse had operational and economic advantages, but even in this field, the horse was giving way to the motor by the end of the decade.

Box vans, of course, were mainly used for 'smalls' and part-loads, but by 1930 most 'tonnage' carriers using open lorries were concentrating on regular routes, to the great advantage of users and themselves. With frequent operation over the same roads, better provision could be made for return traffic and permanent customers could be secured. By comparison with today's vehicles, units were small. A trunk vehicle on a regular run would usually be a 4-tonner perhaps with a 3ton 4-wheel trailer. Collection and delivery vehicles were usually in the 1-2ton category. The build-up of regular services brought about the appearance of that familiar figure in the haulage world, the shunter, because towards the end of the 1920s, improved comfort for the driver and better lighting (electricity instead of oil or acetylene) made night running possible, and, indeed, essential for profitable working in competitive conditions.

The 1920s began a movement to the roads away from other forms of transport besides the railways. Fisher-Renwick, at the end of the decade, began to supplement its London and Manchester steamers by starting services to both Manchester and Liverpool

from London, using large box vans, and in the 1930s these completely superseded the coastal route. Some time last century Arthur Gamman of Chatham started working to London with hoys which discharged at the Thames wharves. Goods brought back were delivered in the Medway towns by horse vans. After 1919, the use of hoys gradually declined and their place was taken by road motors. James W. Cook & Co were London wharfingers and lightermen, who in 1929 started Eastern Roadways with headquarters at Norwich and built up services covering all East Anglia.

The years from 1919 to 1933 were the heyday of the clearing houses or freight brokers, as some of them called themselves. The basic idea was a good one and of great practical value in the early days of uncontrolled operation. It was all very well for an owner-driver to get a load from, say, London to Manchester, but if he did not know anyone in Manchester, what was he to do for a backload? He might waste hours and, perhaps, days enquiring round and then be forced to go home empty. How much better if he could call at an office where there was a list of loads waiting to be collected and where there might be one in the direction he wanted to go.

The necessity to save fuel during World War 1 prompted Manchester Chamber of Commerce in July 1917 to start a clearing house at Parr's Bank Buildings, York Street, Manchester with Nathan Fine as manager. In July 1919 the Chamber ceased to be responsible, but Fine carried on himself. Nottingham Chamber of Commerce also started a clearing house in 1919, with W. Donaldson Wright as manager and this continued as such until the mid 1930s, when it too, ceased to have any connection with its original sponsors.

The most spectacular attempt to open up this field was the taking of the whole of the front page of the *Daily Mail* for 20 May 1922 by the National Road Transport Clearing House Ltd. When the company was registered on 20 April 1921 Robert Carey and W. A. Kemp were given as subscribers. These were named as directors in a return dated 27 October 1921, together with A. M. Davis, G. A. Watkins, H. C. Burdett and C. Barrington. The company was dissolved by court order on 3 July 1923, but the names of Carey, Davis and Barrington appeared again in the next few years as directors of the clearing house called Carey, Davis & Thomas. Claud Barrington, after war service in which he lost a hand, had started with one

lorry in Bristol in 1921, but in the same year joined National as clerk in its Birmingham office. His subsequent career will be referred to later.

Ex-Army Transportation Co was founded in Liverpool in 1919 and changed its name to Ex-Army Transport Ltd in 1928, by which time it had its main base at Manchester. Its founder was J. F. Archbold, whose son, D. K. Archbold, became wellknown after the last war as head of the family clearing house in Leeds. This firm not only gave out traffic but provided financial assistance to men wishing to enter haulage. This was also the practice of many of the clearing houses which proliferated during the 1920s and it was one which led to the whole system being given a bad name. Unscrupulous houses would enter into hire-purchase agreements with newcomers on terms which were onerous in themselves and would, in addition, bind the hirer to accept traffic in the hirer's home town only from the clearing house and on the clearing house's terms. There was no legal limitation on the commission which the clearing house might deduct from the rate paid by the consignor and, in most cases, the man who actually delivered the goods would have no idea of the charge. There must have been hundreds of men who found that the rates they were being paid were so low that, after paying their expenses, they were unable to keep up their hirepurchase instalments and they ended with no lorry and a lost deposit.

This is not to say that there were no honest clearing houses. Walter Gammons of London and Transport Economy of Birmingham, for instance, had a good reputation and no doubt, there were others. In some areas, there were tentative moves to form clearing houses jointly owned by operators, but this was more a development of the 1930s, although Direct Motor Service (Sheffield) Ltd was an early example.

Had there been no unscrupulous persons in the business, clearing houses could have helped to stabilise the industry, secure reasonable rates for hauliers and provide satisfactory services for traders, but there were so many who were not scrupulous that, instead of helping to bring order into the industry, they kept it largely in a state of disorganisation as far as the 'tonnage' section was concerned. Hauliers themselves were not entirely blameless, even those who were not officially in the clearing house business. An operator would accept a load for a place he did not intend to go to and then try to farm it out. A second operator would accept it and then himself pass it on. Each time, the rate offered would decrease so that when eventually the traffic was moved, the man who did the job got many shillings a ton less than the trader paid out. This nefarious practice, which continued well into the 1930s, had its amusing side. It was not unknown for the traffic to be offered back to the firm which originally accepted the order after it had been through three or four hands, with a certain amount being deducted from the rate each time.

37

Chapter 5

A Royal Commission on Transport under the chairmanship of Sir Arthur Griffith Boscawen, set up in 1928, issued two reports in 1929, which formed the basis of the Road Traffic Act, 1930. The most dramatic result of this Act was the introduction of a nationwide system of licensing passenger-carrying vehicles by traffic commissioners. It did not, in practice, greatly affect hauliers, although there was one section (19) which should have done, because it limited drivers' hours. This section is set out in appendix 1. In practice the section was unenforceable in haulage at that time as there was no obligation on operators to keep records of hours worked.

Motor vehicles were classified into: (a) heavy locomotives, weighing unladen more than $11\frac{1}{2}$ton; (b) light locomotives, weighing unladen not more than $11\frac{1}{2}$ton; (c) motor tractors, weighing unladen not more than $7\frac{1}{4}$ton; (d) heavy motor cars, weighing unladen not more than $2\frac{1}{2}$ton and (e) motor cars, besides (f) motorcycles and (g) invalid carriages. Trailers were to be limited to one behind a motor car or heavy motor car, but a motor tractor might draw one laden and two unladen trailers.

Severe speed limits were imposed. Heavy locomotives were limited to 3mph in built-up areas, otherwise to 5mph; light locomotives with not more than two trailers to 8mph with 'soft or elastic tyres', otherwise to 5mph; heavy motor cars and motor tractors 16mph; other goods vehicles 20mph if on pneumatic tyres and not drawing a trailer; if on 'soft or elastic' tyres 16mph; with a trailer, 16mph if the trailer had pneumatic tyres, otherwise 12mph.

Persons under 17 were not to drive a motor car and persons under 21 were not to drive a locomotive, tractor or heavy motor car. When a goods vehicle was drawing a trailer a second man was to be carried to attend to the trailer. (This provision was made because trailer brakes were usually then cable-operated from the cab of the drawing vehicle and applying them was a separate operation from applying the footbrake.)

Tests were to be instituted before the grant of driving licences, and third-party insurance became compulsory. Provision was made for charging drivers with reckless, dangerous or careless driving or driving when under the influence of drink or drugs. The Minister was given power to make regulations controlling the construction and use of motor vehicles.

The Commission in its next and final report, published in January, 1931, urged that the proceeds of motor taxation should be used solely for highway maintenance and improvement and should not be used for the general purposes of government. (At the time of the report, the Road Fund had only been 'raided' and not absorbed into the general revenue. The taxation of road vehicles started in 1909 with a tax of 3d a gallon on petrol. The Finance Act, 1920, abolished this duty and replaced it by a scale based on unladen weight [goods vehicles] or seats [passenger vehicles], but the petrol tax was reimposed in 1928 at 4d a gallon. The Local Government Act, 1929 gave rating relief to the railways and to farmers and the additional taxation on road vehicles was intended to help finance this.) The railways' lack of enterprise was strongly criticised, but the Commission, nevertheless, considered that it was not in the public interest that there should be a further diversion of heavy goods traffic to road. For this reason it considered that no heavy motor car should be allowed to exceed 10ton unladen, with a maximum laden weight of 4ton on any wheel. It preferred that, in general, 4ton unladen should be the maximum and that the use of vehicles above that weight should be penalised by taxation.

The Commission consulted the Transport & General Workers' Union, the National Road Transport Employers' Federation, the Long Distance Road Haulage Committee of Inquiry and the Commercial Motor Users' Association about the advisability of licensing hauliers. The CMUA, representing mainly the ancillary users, was opposed to any form of licensing; the other bodies were 'strongly in favour'. (Although this may have been the official view, many hauliers, despite the intense competition, were not in favour.) The Commission thought that a simple system would suffice. All that would be necessary for a licence would be that the vehicles employed should be in a fit condition and that the employees' wages should be satisfactory.

But before the government did anything about licensing, the industry was subjected to another enquiry. A committee under the chairmanship of Sir Arthur Salter, called the Conference on Rail & Road Transport, was set up following a meeting which P. J.

Above: *Passing through the outskirts of Dunstable in June 1936 en route from Brierley Hill, Staffs, to London, two Scammell articulators carrying parts of a gasometer out-of-gauge for the railways; Mr Leavesley evidently named his lorries, as the loading one is inscribed 'Fig Leaf'! note the chain driven rear wheels of the tractor, each, apparently, with four solid tyres.*

Right: *Sir Alfred Salter, an eminent civil servant was appointed in 1932 to chair a conference which tried to assess vehicle costs in relation to road wear; it recommended staggering increases in commercial motor taxation.*

Pybus, then Minister of Transport, had with representatives of the Railway Companies Association, the Standing Joint Committee of Mechanical Road Transport Associations and the Long Distance Road Haulage Association on 21 March 1932. The railway representatives on the committee were the chairmen of the four amalgamated railway companies, Sir Herbert Walker (SR), Sir James Milne (GWR), Sir Ralph Wedgwood (LNER) and Sir Josiah Stamp (LMSR). The road representatives, all appointed by the Standing Joint

Above: *As Surrey Docks specialised in the import of timber and the lorry belonged to a Millwall firm, one must assume that the tremendous length of wood had travelled by road from London to Southampton; did it have a police escort? curious that there are no markers on the ends of the beam!*

Below: *Saurer was once a common name in lorry fleets; Dyson, the trailer-manufacturer, associated with Saurer in this combination, is still in existence; the Medway Oil & Storage Co Ltd ordered five of these in 1925; four had four separate tanks each; this one was designed to carry cans as well as loose fuel; it was designed for a 12ton load; note the drop frame and hinged legs; the address in the Isle of Grain is interesting; this was 25 years before the giant refinery was started.*

Committee, were W. H. Gaunt, distribution manager of J. Lyons Ltd; C. le M. Gosselin, managing director of H. Viney and Co Ltd of Preston and a past-president of the Commercial Motor Users' Association; P. R. Turner, managing director of Thomas Allen Ltd, president of the London Haulage Contractors' Association and E. Graham Guest, president of the Scottish Commercial Motor Users' Association. The Minister did not lay down terms of reference, but the subjects to be considered were agreed at the meeting by those present. When the Conference's report was published, it was obvious that it had covered a much wider field than was envisaged at the March meeting.

The Long Distance Road Haulage Association (which, about this time, changed its name to the Road Haulage Association) strongly resented the government's refusal to allow it representation on the conference on the ground that the SJC adequately represented the haulage industry. It was not even allowed to send its chairman (E. C. Marston) to expound the association's viewpoint, but had to content itself with putting in a written statement. As the conference was intended to examine the effect of

Above: *Anybody knowledgeable in transport history will automatically connect Gilford with fast passenger chassis of which a great many were sold to London independents in 'the roaring twenties'; E. B. Horne got an agency for the American Garford in 1925 and then launched Gilford, buying all the parts from different makers; before production ceased in 1937, some 2,700 vehicles had been sold, amongst them a few 50cwt tippers like this one.*

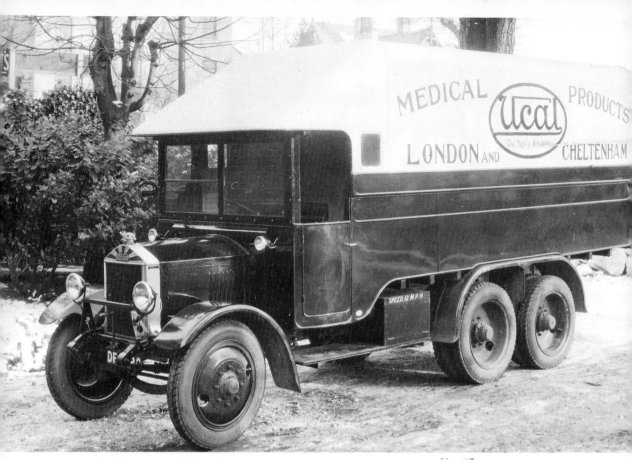

the development of road transport on the economy, and to consider what could be done to improve the organisation of the industry, the annoyance of the association is understandable, since it certainly represented more of the long-distance professional hauliers than the SJC. The passenger transport section was equally offended when it saw that, without being given an opportunity to express its reactions, it was likely to be subjected to increased taxation.

Although the conference, like the Royal Commission before it, accepted that a mathematically sound formula to relate highway expenditure to the use of the roads by motor vehicles could not be worked out, it nevertheless suggested a scale of taxation for each class of vehicle which should have as its object the payment by motor users of the whole cost of the roads, said then to be £60,000,000 a year, irrespective of their use by others. Apart from pedestrians, there were still great numbers of horse-drawn vehicles in use. The railway companies alone, at December 1931, owned 31,188 horse-drawn vehicles.

Having decided that motor users ought to pay £60,000,000 a year the conference tried to ascertain the ton-mileage per year of the different classes of vehicles and their fuel consumption and, on figures

Above: Besides turning out 6-wheelers to get a better distribution of axle-loads in this country the War Office inspired makers to build small machines of this type which could be used on the rough roads of colonial territories; a great many Albions were sold abroad, but the company also produced models for the home market like this 4-tonner which had both rear-axles driven; the frame was peculiar, as it was high and level above the rear-wheels and then dropped under the cab and bonnet.

which were no more than guesswork, decided that commercial goods vehicles ought to pay £23½ million a year, leaving all other motor vehicles to pay £36½ million, regardless of the fact that, at that time, the heavier types of commercial vehicles were usually only to be found on class 1 and class 2 roads, which totalled 42,995 miles compared with 133,796 miles of unclassified road.

The 23½ million was £2½ million more than was being collected by excise licences and the petrol duty of 8d a gallon. Vehicles driven by steam, electricity or compression-ignition engines paid no duty on their motive power. The scale of excise duties stopped at 5ton unladen weight.

The conference, therefore, recommended that all forms of mechanically-propelled goods vehicles on the roads should be called on for an increased contribution to the cost of them. The following are some examples of the figures in the scale it suggested:

Propulsion	Weight not exceeding	Annual duty	
		Existing £	Proposed £
Internal combustion (petrol)	2½ ton (on pneumatics)	28	33
	5	43	73
	10	48	226
Internal combustion other than petrol	2½ ton	28	64
	5	43	134
	10	48	332
Steam	2½	28	58
	5	43	112
	10	48	170

These proposals, of course, were hotly contested by the road transport men, but they were forced through by the government. One might have supposed that the change to ci engines as the principal motive power for heavy vehicles would have been held up or even stopped, by the tremendous increase in taxation, but the greater mileage per gallon given by the 'diesel', ensured its ever-increasing use. Steam, on the other hand, was hit badly and its final decline can be dated from the acceptance of the report.

The Royal Commission, it will be remembered, considered that licensing of goods vehicles should be limited to securing the fitness of vehicles and the payment of reasonable wages. The RHA accepted this view and added that regard should be had to the 'general suitability of an applicant (for a licence) in the matter of knowledge of the business and resources to conduct it'. It rejected absolutely all suggestion of route or commodity control and, while agreeing that

Below: *Latil, a French firm, first appeared in the British market in 1923; it specialised in tractors with both 4-wheel drive and 4-wheel steering, but it also designed general purpose vehicles with low floors; this small B type lorry, new in 1927, had a dropped frame at the rear to give a height from the ground of only 18in; the back axle was dead and the drive was from a differential with transverse output shafts carrying pinions at the outer ends; these engaged large gearwheels which were, in effect, the rear brake drums.*

an ancillary user should be free to carry his own goods without a haulier's licence, considered that he ought to apply for one if he proposed to carry 'for hire or reward'.

The Road & Rail Traffic Act, 1933 came into force on 1 January 1934 and completely changed the outlook for the road transport of goods. It made the operation of goods vehicles, whether for hire or reward or for ancillary purposes, illegal except under one of three classes of licence. The 'A' licence was for 'public carriers', the 'B' licence for 'limited carriers' and the 'C' licence for 'private carriers'. The 'C' licensee was not allowed to carry any goods for hire or reward; the holder of a 'B' licence might carry either his own or any other person's goods. If he chose to carry for others, the Licensing Authority (who was, in fact, the Chairman of Traffic Commissioners under the 1930 Act) might attach such conditions as he thought fit in respect of the type of goods to be carried or the customers for whom they might be carried or the places to which they might be carried. Every licence had to specify the registration marks and unladen weights of the authorised vehicles plus the number and unladen weights of trailers authorised (if any).

'A' licences were originally issued for two years, 'B' for one year and 'C' for three, but these periods were later increased to five, two and five years respectively. Provision was made for the issue of short term licences for work of limited duration or pending a decision on a substantive licence. 'C' licences were to be granted automatically, subject to satisfactory conduct in regard to vehicle maintenance and drivers' hours. 'A' licensees were given the right to receive a similar licence where they could prove the existence of a contract to provide vehicles for the exclusive use of a particular hirer other than another carrier. Vehicles used for agricultural work and certain special types for

municipal work were exempt from licensing. An operator applying for an 'A' or 'B' licence not later than 1 April 1934, who could prove that he was using vehicles for hire or reward in the year beginning 1 April 1932, was given the right to a licence for tonnage not exceeding the tonnage he had in use during that year.

It has been mentioned in connection with the 1930 Act that section 19, restricting the hours of work by drivers, was virtually unenforceable for goods transport because of the absence of records. The 1933 Act sought to remedy this by imposing on operators the obligation to keep records and on drivers to carry the approved forms with them. Thus started the 'log sheets', which were a source of trouble to conscientious operators for the next 35 years. It was often more difficult to get properly filled in sheets back from drivers than to get the work done and there was the constant fear that the sheets might not truthfully reflect a driver's meal breaks or hours of rest. Many hauliers were convicted of 'aiding and abetting' breaches of the hours regulations when the offending drivers were many miles from base and it was impossible to supervise their actions. On the other hand, the enforcement officers of the Ministry had a continuous battle with unscrupulous owners and drivers who falsified the sheets.

Objections to an application for a licence could be lodged by:

'Persons who are already providing facilities, whether by means of road transport or any other kind of transport, for the carriage of goods for hire or reward in the district, or between the places, which the applicant intends to serve, on the ground that suitable transport facilities in that district, or between those places, are or, if the application were granted, would be, either generally or in respect of any particular type of vehicles, in excess of requirements, or on the ground that any of the conditions of a licence held by the applicant has not been complied with'.

An operator wishing to appeal against a decision of the Traffic Commissioners under the 1930 Act had to apply to the Minister, who appointed an inspector to review the case, and then gave a decision granting or

Left: *The American International Harvester Company introduced its 2¼ton Speed Truck in the mid-20s and, as was not unusual at that time, some users ordered extensions; Eagle Engineering of Warwick produced this one.*

Below: *Vulcan, based at Southport, was one of the earliest motor manufacturers; in 1926 it was offering a choice ranging from this 7cwt van to a 4-tonner, as well as chassis for buses; £295 complete with electric lighting and starter, was the price for this neat little job with 4-wheel brakes (only just coming in then) and worm-driven rear axle.*

rejecting the operator's plea. This is still the procedure today with passenger appeals, but when licensing for goods vehicles was under consideration there was agitation against this system. It was contended that the Minister ought not to be both judge and jury and that appeals should be heard by an independent body. The government accepted this proposal and the 1933 Act provided for the establishment of an Appeal Tribunal, with power to take evidence on oath and to award costs, if it thought fit, against any of the parties to an appeal. The Tribunal's decisions were made binding on licensing authorities. The effect of the Tribunal on the industry will be discussed later.

The railways at this time were subject to legislation which had been introduced when they had a monopoly of long distance traffic. They had to work to a classification imposed by the Railways Act, 1921, and to apply the standard charges laid down in the classification, unless authorised to grant exceptional rates by the Railway Rates Tribunal, which was also established by the 1921 Act. To avoid a charge of 'undue preference' an exceptional rate, if authorised, had to be offered to all traders in similar

Above: *The Star Engineering Co, originally the Star Cycle Co, passed under Guy control in 1928 and after 1931 the name disappeared; the company was better known as a maker of fast passenger chassis and, at one time, of touring cars, but in 1927 it offered 15cwt, 25cwt and 30cwt vans, similar to this example for Lucas.*

circumstances. From the earliest days, railway rates had been based on 'what the traffic will bear' which meant that commodities of high intrinsic value were charged more per mile than commodities of lower value. Specially low rates were in force for basic raw materials. Railway rates did not reflect the cost of operation per unit, because such a calculation would have been (and is) impossible, since the cost of the track which is the basis of railway operation cannot be attributed precisely to any particular parcel of traffic (or any individual passenger) passing over it.

Road transport costs (except for parcels traffic) can be calculated with fair precision for each consignment moved and this gave the road operators a great advantage. The high value goods in the top classes of the railway classification rarely moved in anywhere near full wagon loads and were particularly susceptible to road competition, as hauliers could offer much lower rates and still make a profit.

The 1933 Act gave the railways power, subject to the consent of the Rates Tribunal, to enter into an arrangement with a trader to carry the whole or part of his traffic at an 'agreed charge', which the railways, in practice, interpreted as offering a flat rate. This was a powerful weapon in their fight against the hauliers, which their commercial staffs exploited to the full.

The railways took full advantage of their powers of objection to licence applications and for the first year or two almost every application for a new licence or for additional vehicles or for an extension of the conditions attached to a 'B' licence was opposed. It was not permissible to replace vehicles already

Above: *L. Walkley combined a daily parcel service between the Forest of Dean and Gloucester with household removals and the versatile Bedford with ample 'luton' was just the job.*

licensed by others of a larger weight without authority, unless the increase were negligible, and many a haulier became involved in a strenuous fight in the traffic court for this reason, even when he did not want to add to the number of his vehicles.

When the Bill which became the Act was under consideration, the then Minister of Transport (P. J. Pybus) made it clear that 'B' licences were intended solely for part-time hauliers having another business as well, such as coal merchants. Nevertheless, it was a regular part of railway tactics to suggest to applicants that there would be no railway objection if they would change the application to one for a 'B' licence with the proposed user set out clearly. Many hauliers succumbed to this suggestion and thereby gave away their birthright. Applicants for 'A' licences had to state the proposed normal user but, as no conditions could be attached to an 'A' licence, no offence was committed if an operator changed his route or the type of goods he carried. All that could happen would be that he might be challenged when his licence expired and might fail to obtain a renewal. Conditions attached to a 'B' licence, by contrast, were enforceable and an operator could be prosecuted for breaking them. Oddly enough, although some perspicacious hauliers refused to be trapped, this misuse of the 'B' licence was never stopped until after the period covered by this book, not in fact until 1964.

The railways not only objected at the licensing authorities' public enquiries, but frequently pursued their objections by appeal to the Tribunal. Although this was frequently vexatious and extremely expensive

47

for hauliers, it actually did good in the long run, because cases were decided in which the principles laid down enabled the industry to achieve a much higher degree of organisation in the fourth decade of the century than in the previous 10 years.

The Act set out the criteria for granting an 'A' or 'B' licence in section 6(2) which said 'The licensing authority in exercising his discretion shall have regard primarily to the interests of the public generally, including those of persons requiring, as well as those of persons providing, facilities for transport'.

The Tribunal tended generally to stress the requirements of traders as having more weight than the interests of transport users. This was notably so in the experience of H. W. Hawker Ltd of Bristol which ran between there and Lancashire, where the company had a depot at Warrington. It specialised in the conveyance of bacon for the many curers in Wiltshire and Gloucestershire and had to appeal three times against the refusal of additional vehicles as the traffic grew. What happened is illustrative of the delays which often occurred especially when an appeal was made. Hawker, who started his business in 1924, made it into a limited company in September 1934 and the 'A' licence then in force was transferred without difficulty. When the company applied in February 1935 for further vehicles it was refused and thereupon appealed. The appeal was successful, but not till May. The following February (1936) more vehicles were applied for and again refused. This time the decision of the Appeal Tribunal, again favourable to Hawker, was not given until December, 1936. There then followed five months during which Hawker was trying to obtain

Left: *At the top of the Foden range, an 8-wheeler with 6-cylinder Gardner engine capable of carrying 15½ton; Mileham's lorries were a familiar sight in London's Dockland.*

Above: *What was the spare wheel doing on the pavement when this picture was taken?; it shows a 6-8ton Fordson tractor, hauling a Dyson semi-trailer with a loading height of only 2ft 7½in from the ground, the rear axle has four wheels in line on twins; Cliffords specialised in moving machinery.*

a renewal of licences in both the Western and North-Western traffic areas. With this cleared up, the company applied on 16 July 1937 for further additions to the fleet. The case was not heard until mid-September when it took up three days, and even then the Licensing Authority did not give his decision which was adverse until 10 December 1937. Hawker appealed again, but the appeal was not heard until the following May. The main ground of the appeal was that the Licensing Authority had attempted to lay down a rule that if traders in Lancashire wanted bacon they could not have it if there were bacon producers in Lancashire. The case was notorious for the vast number of documents and statistics demanded by the Authority, which led eventually to the applicant refusing to supply any more.

As it was said above, an 'A' licence could not have conditions attached to it, but an operator was not entitled to an automatic renewal at the expiry of a licence and this gave potential objectors a chance. In the case of the Four Amalgamated Railway Companies v Bouts-Tillotson Transport in 1937, it was laid down that proof had to be given that the vehicles had been regularly and fully used and that there had been no material change in the business. In another Bouts-Tillotson case and also in the case of GW and LMS Railway Companies v Smart (1938), the Tribunal agreed that operators of regular services were entitled to a reasonable number of collection and delivery vehicles at the termini of their trunk routes.

Left: *Henry Garner built lorries in Moseley, Birmingham, from an early date but after his firm was absorbed by Sentinel of Shrewsbury in 1935, there was a decline and in 1939 production ceased; although this model had a 6-cylinder engine and twin rear tyres it was only designed to carry 2ton.*

Below left: *After nearly a century as canal and road carriers in Birmingham and the Black Country, Picton & Co collapsed under the strain of war and sold out in 1943 to Central Carriers, a subsidiary of PX and Young's Express.*

Below: *Leyland Beaver tractors with fuel tanks passing through the Avon Gorge.*

This decision was of particular importance to the carriers of parcels and smalls, who normally have more collection and delivery vehicles than trunkers. The case of Boston Haulage Co Ltd and Sanderson v London & North Eastern Railway Co in 1936 involved the purchase of a business by Boston Haulage (a clearing house) from one of its sub-contractors. It was held that there could be no element of goodwill in such a case, but that a licence could be granted to the purchaser if there were proof of sufficient traffic having been carried on a sound financial basis to justify the number of vehicles to be taken over and if those traders for whom the sub-contractor had regularly carried were prepared to continue their use of the service.

Chapter 6

The carriage of parcels and small consignments by road over considerable distances was a well-established facility in this country long before the railway era. By 1637, when John Taylor of London compiled *The Carriers' Cosmography,* almost the whole of England and Wales was connected with London by carrier services, despite the frightful condition of the roads. Many places then had a direct service to London which they lost with the development of railways and have never regained.

Most of these early carriers were based in the provinces and worked into London, putting up for a night or two at some inn in the city or suburbs, where parcels could be received. (The tradition of 'carriers' quarters' in the cities continued in Scotland until the 1940s.) The stage coaches, which began regular operation in the late 17th century, and the mail coaches, which started in 1784, undertook the conveyance of small urgent packages, but it was not until a national railway network was built up that provincial carriers ceased to operate into London.

There remained a great number working from villages into market towns and, because the railway companies were reluctant to provide collection and delivery facilities, many of these developed as feeders to the railways and distributors for them. In all major towns agents sprang up who were prepared to collect and deliver railborne parcels. Some of these firms opened branches in more than one town so that such names as Sutton & Co, Atlas Express and Sanderson became nationally well known.

At the same time as railway expansion encouraged the growth of such firms, the spread of large towns beyond the radius of the handcart brought the need for delivery services by horse-drawn vehicles. Thus came about the rise of Carter, Paterson in London from 1860 and the institution of Pickford's and McNamara's local services in the metropolis. Pickford and McNamara had both been long-distance carriers before the railways came.

Outside London, the expansion of the industrial towns beyond convenient walking distances not only demanded improved local transport for goods but for passengers, too. This demand was met first by horse-buses and then from the 1870s largely by tramcars, either horse-drawn or steam hauled. Many local bus and tram companies carried parcels and this practice was continued when most urban services were municipalised about the turn of the century. The British Electric Traction group, as it built new electric tramways, also developed parcels services.

The most notable of the municipal parcels services was that of Manchester, which at an early date supplemented the tram service with deliveries and collections by van, interchanged traffic with surrounding municipalities and was a forwarding agent for parcels by rail.

Thus the positon at the end of World War 1 was that there were many local carrier services, urban and rural, for parcels and smalls, but no trunk services operating by road. In 1919, McNamara started 'smalls' services from London to Birmingham, Liverpool, Bradford and Bristol, but its example was not immediately followed. McNamara had had experience of motor operation over what were then long distances for mechanical traction since 1906, when its Post Office contract run from London to Slough was motorised.

The development of regular long distance parcels services was really due to provincial carriers working into London and, in particular, the offer of carriers in Leicestershire and Northamptonshire to carry boots 'loose', ie in one-pair cartons instead of in large cartons and cases. Because this traffic required vans (instead of open lorries), they were able also to carry high value hosiery in safety and at much lower rates than when it was railborne. The use of vans also made it practicable to carry return loads of smalls.

Other parts of the country were slower to develop in this way. Smalls traffic requires terminal facilities superior to those necessary for handling tonnage, entails much more documentation and needs more staff. Consequently, those who flooded into the industry in the early 1920s mostly steered clear of it. Handling full loads was much easier. The smalls carriers were not free from problems, and one of the most difficult of these was to deliver or collect individual parcels over the wide area of London and other major conurbations.

Rather strangely, although Birmingham was called the city of a thousand trades and the Black Country too, was noted for its hundreds of small factories, there

Above: *For generations Carter, Paterson, founded in 1860, was the principal parcel carrier in London, with a number of depots between which transfer vans were run; in the late 1920s it developed the use of lift-bodies, which were often moved about, as in this picture, in pairs (getting badly knocked about in the process, apparently).*

was no development of regular services in the 1920s corresponding to those in the East Midlands. Half way through the decade there were scores of lorries running up and down between Birmingham and London but they were nearly all on a tramping basis, getting traffic when and where they could and only handling tonnage. McNamara alone at this time gave a regular and properly organised service for parcels and small lots on this route, but there was an interesting newcomer on the A45 and A5 in the late 1920s — new to trunking, but, in fact, an old business.

In 1836, Joseph Brevitt, a Willenhall locksmith, started walking to Birmingham, 11 miles away, on Saturdays, to deliver the locks he had made during the week. Before long he was asked to deliver for other people and replaced his packhorse by a cart. His son, Josiah, joined him at the age of eight and some time towards the end of the century, father and son stopped making keys and concentrated on carrying. By 1914,

the Brevitt family owned over 40 vehicles. The pick of their horses were commandeered for the army and most of their men left for the forces, so Josiah (then 64) decided to confine his work to travelling to and from Wolverhampton with a solitary horse and cart.

His daughter had married a Willenhall man named Rissbrook and their son, Fred, born in 1903, determined from his earliest days to be a carrier. When he was 17 he obtained a driving licence and persuaded his grandfather to buy a T-model Ford, which was used to provide a regular service to Birmingham and,

53

Left: *City & Suburban, working from Stepney Green, continued a separate existence as a local London carrier after its purchase by Carter, Paterson; it favoured the 40-50cwt Dennis, with cab doors forward of the front-axle.*

Below left: *N. Francis & Co Ltd an old-established parcel carrier in north-east London retained its independence until after World War 2; the body on this Dennis, designed for 40-45cwt, was specially built to give the driver easy egress because of the numerous stops entailed in parcel work; in 1934, when this picture was taken, Dennis had a very wide range — not only freight vehicles but also buses, fire-engines, gulley-emptiers and other municipal vehicles.*

Right: *E. B. Hutchinson was one of the outstanding bus men of the 1920s; he started United Automobile Services at Lowestoft in 1912 and later created a network of services in Northumberland, Durham and Cleveland; he sold almost all his passenger interests to the London & North Eastern Railway in 1929 and then invested in haulage, notably Ryburn United Transport, which he later sold to the Hanson and Holdsworth group.*

before the end of the decade, as the fleet grew, to London also. When it became necessary to have a delivery and collection agent in London, Brevitts began working with Allied Freight Services.

In 1928, the ambiguous position of the four amalgamated railway companies as carriers of goods and passengers by road was settled and they received powers to run collection and delivery services and to operate buses. For the most part they bought or obtained an interest in existing bus services rather than start new ones and among their acquisitions was United Automobile Services with an extensive network in Northumberland, Durham and East Anglia. This purchase meant that E. B. Hutchinson, the man who had created United, was out of the bus business, except for a small coaching firm. He decided to invest in haulage and brought together several small businesses (including a bodybuilder and trailer manufacturer) as Ryburn United Transport, based on Leeds.

United had carried parcels and Hutchinson knew about the bulk carriage of parcels by rail for firms who provided local delivery services. The idea occurred to him of starting trunk services linking the industrial towns and for this purpose, in 1929, he launched Transport Service Ltd with L. W. Morton, who had been employed by Lincolnshire Road Car Co, as director and manager. Transport Service was not to

engage in collection and delivery but only to trunk. It should not be confused with the later Transport Services, Ltd which became the holding company of a large group.

Services operating six days a week were started to Newcastle-upon-Tyne, London, Birmingham, Manchester and Liverpool. Hutchinson had his eyes even further afield. A pamphlet date April 1933 said:

'Special through traffic arrangements are now in operation with the chief Air Services starting from London, and which now cover almost all Europe, and also extend to Egypt, Persia, India, as well as Central and South Africa.

'Goods entrusted to the Company for these services are handed over to the air carriers immediately on arrival in London and are placed on the next plane despatched.'

It is interesting to note that a 6lb parcel could be collected in Bradford or Leeds and carried to the aerodrome at Cape Town for 41s 5d with a transit time of 12 days from London. For Paris, the transit time from London was three hours and the cost for 6lb, 4s 11d including delivery within city limits.

By the time this pamphlet was published, however, Transport Service was in dissolution and, during 1933, faded out completely as an effective organisation.

Ryburn United continued to run long distance services but on the more usual lines of working only between its own depots and handling medium weights rather than parcels and smalls.

Transport Service failed for three reasons. It could not maintain a regular service, it could not assimilate the greatly varying rates structures of the other carriers with whom it worked and it did not evolve an easy method of recording and accounting.

Possibly the Manchester and Liverpool services might have worked with a reasonable degree of regularity, but the others had too many stops. Birmingham was served by a van which started at Bradford and called at Leeds, Barnsley, Sheffield, Chesterfield and Derby. It is a feature of parcel carrying that the operator never knows in advance how much traffic he has to handle and consequently the time required to unload and/or load at stops is almost unpredictable.

The Transport Service driver was expected to do the round trip, Bradford-Birmingham-Bradford, within the 11 hours maximum prescribed in the Road Traffic Act, 1930, but this was impossible and the service ran later and later, sometimes missing a day altogether.

Where Transport Service went wrong on rates was in publishing a scale of through charges from collection to delivery, according to mileage. Had the whole transaction been within Transport Service's control this might have been practicable, but all that Transport Service controlled was the trunking. The co-operating carriers were supposed to charge through traffic to their customers on the Transport Service schedule, but the charges they themselves put against Tranport Service were not necessarily the same as the trunking carrier had allowed in building up its rates. Had Transport Service charged the sending carrier a bulk tonnage rate for trunking, instead of calculating every parcel separately, and left the local carriers to settle direct for the terminal work, much clerical labour would have been saved and the trunk rate could have been adjusted in the light of operating experience. As it was, the clerical work involved was very heavy, since Transport Service had to price every individual consignment and credit the collection and delivery agents.

There was a curious situation in Birmingham at this time. Several carriers came into the city from the suburbs and, as in the coaching days, parked their vans in the yards of certain public houses. At one time there had been an internal service by a private firm

Left: A 1937 Bedford to carry 50cwt in the Red Arrow London fleet.

Below: On 28 September 1937, the author invited all the parcel carriers with whom his firm (Red Arrow Deliveries) worked to send representatives to a meeting in Birmingham, which led to the formation, on 8 November 1937, of the National Conference of Parcel Carriers, later renamed the National Conference of Express Carriers and now the Express Carriers functional group in the Road Haulage Association; during the September gathering those present inspected the Red Arrow depot at Yardley. Seen here are (left to right):
L. B. Austin (City & Suburban), W. H. Stocks (RA), E. Burton (United Automobile Services), W. H. West (Donaldson Wright), W. C. Ball (Bradford-Leicester Transport), J. J. Marshall, junr (Marshall, Son and Reading), G. Gripton (Pickfords), A. A. Hammond (RA), A. S. Onion (Pickfords), D. Maclachlan (Globe Parcels Express), R. Sephton (Blackburn Parcels Express), — Martin (Globe), H. R. Gore (Blackburn PE), J. Gee (Dawsons), I. R. Macalister (Carter, Paterson), W. H. Taylor (Kent Carriers), A. Packlam (London and Southern Counties), H. Bridges, W. J. A. Peck (PX) F. D. Hulse, J. W. Beresford (Beresford, Caddy and Pemberton), L. Walkley, D. Richardson (Gamman and Dicker), A. W. Bredemear and C. S. Dunbar (RA), W. H. Bexon (Donaldson Wright), F. Platts (Platts Bros), E. D. Peck (PX), F. S. Huxham, W. Tombs (Cheltenham Traction), B. C. Medlen (Huxham & Company), J. R. Farmer (RA), W. D. Hulse, F. S. Huxham, junr, A. Myers (Bradford-Leicester), W. B. Allsop (Derby Express), R. B. Brittain (National Parcels), W. Hunter (Beresford, Caddy and Pemberton), J. P. Young (Young's Express); the man obscured by W. Tombs is either C. Sanderson (Henson) or K. Lamb (Lep)

covering the whole city as it was before the great extension of 1912, but by the 1920s this had faded out.

It had been replaced by facilities provided by the Birmingham & Midland Motor Omnibus Company (the Midland Red), which, besides carrying parcels on its buses developed a fleet of vans. These were originally intended for use inside Birmingham only, but, in a short time, services were being run to Coventry and Worcester and later to Stoke-on-Trent, to connect with the parcels service of the Potteries Electric Traction Co. The Birmingham & Midland Tramways Joint Committee operated three box cars for goods which ran every weekday over the extensive Black Country tramway network. When the trams were abandoned the Midland Red parcel vans took over the work. At about the time the railway companies secured control of Carter, Paterson, the London parcels carriers, (1933), that company had begun to expand, partly by running its vehicles further afield and partly by the use of railborne containers. The Midland Red agreed to accept two containers a day via Great Western and to reload them back to London each night.

With such a set-up, it was inevitable that Midland Red should also be asked to act for Transport Service. E. A. Mellor was then parcels superintendent of Midland Red. Starting in the Potteries, he had been chosen by the BET to set up parcels systems in all its subsidiaries (which, for a time, included the South Metropolitan Electric Tramways in London). Mellor agreed to take on the Transport Service work, but how

to handle it was left to me. I was then superintendent of the Midland Red depot in Seymour Street, Birmingham.

After 11 years in newspapers, mainly as a circulation and transport manager, I had joined Midland Red in 1930 to widen my transport experience. After some months on general traffic duties, I had been sent to reorganise the working of the Seymour Street depot and found it so hopelessly congested and incapable of extension that it was difficult to give a reliable service. I pressed for better premises and suggested, in the summer of 1933, that although Hutchinson's efforts had not been successful, a nationwide service for parcels and smalls might be organised on a different basis. I had in mind the area agreements which gave the large bus companies spheres of influence and visualised the linking together by jointly-operated trunk services of all the parcels services of the BET, Tilling and Balfour, Beatty groups, plus those of the large municipal undertakings.

My proposals were given scant attention, because the railway companies which had obtained control of Midland Red, were hesitant about allowing it to expand in goods carrying. Eventually, in 1934, Midland Red was ordered to transfer its van services to Pickfords, whose Birmingham furniture repository was developed into a parcels depot.

Before this, however, I had sounded two Birmingham hauliers about the possibility of financing the creation of a nationwide parcels system on the basis of area agreements, not between bus companies, but between parcels carriers. The hauliers were A. Neely, who carried general traffic, mainly to London, and Hurst & Payne, who were mainly concerned with traffic for the Goodyear Tyre Company, usually to or from London and Liverpool. Both were interested, but I decided that Hurst & Payne offered the best prospects.

Their attraction was four-fold. They had a large warehouse at Yardley, giving 32,000 sq ft of unimpeded movement with a glazed roof held up with only one row of stanchions. It had been bought for use as a storage space for rubber which Goodyear had stockpiled, but this was going out quickly and would not be replaced. Hurst & Payne also had considerable 'claimed tonnage'. The Road & Rail Traffic Act, 1933, was to come into force on 1 January 1934. Whole-time hauliers who were in business on 1 April 1932 were entitled to a grant under the new Act of tonnage (unladen weight) equal to the gross tonnage they owned at that date. Hurst & Payne, owing to the falling off in the Goodyear traffic, could claim a much greater tonnage of carrier's licences than they had vehicles. Besides this, they had reasonable repair facilities. They also had an office in London, which might be of value in building up the organisation.

Right: With a totally enclosed area of 32,000 sq ft and an island deck 300ft long, the Red Arrow depot at Yardley, Birmingham was, in the early 1930s, the largest among road carriers outside London entirely devoted to parcels and 'smalls'; both these pictures were taken in 1938, one at about 8.15am on a week day when the local vans were being loaded and the other on a Sunday morning; all drivers wore overalls and peaked caps; the construction of the deck was somewhat unusual; parallel brick walls were built, across which heavy timber bearers were laid at right-angles; on top of these, longitudinal planking was placed; the deck, which was faced with timber, projected beyond the external walls to prevent them being damaged by vans backing in with their tailboards down.

It was, therefore, arranged that a £100 company should be formed to which Hurst & Payne would lend £500. They would let the warehouse to the new company at a rent that would increase as the deck and offices were extended and would buy five vans (four 30cwt and one 2ton) on Bedford chassis with locally-built box bodies, which would be hired. Hurst & Payne also agreed to provide the trunk service to London.

I left Midland Red on 17 November 1933 and Red Arrow Deliveries, Ltd started business on 28 December. Although some work at the depot had been done while I was working out my month's notice and the vans had been ordered, I had, in the short space of six weeks, with Christmas intervening, to arrange the first carrier contacts, have publicity matter printed and distributed, obtain the first customers and engage staff. Curiously enough, the very first parcel ever handled by Red Arrow was one collected from the Midland Red for some place they did not serve.

Most fortunately, just as I had decided to leave Midland Red an enquiry was received from Blackburn Parcels Express, asking if Midland Red would be interested in delivering and collecting for them. The congestion at Seymour Street made it necessary to decline, but seizing the opportunity, I revealed my plans to the management at Blackburn in confidence and it was arranged that Red Arrow, when it started, and Blackburn Parcels would each run a trunk vehicle between the two depots and act as each other's agent. Neely, already mentioned, was invited to supply Red Arrow with a trunk vehicle painted in the company's livery for this purpose.

The original intention was that Red Arrow should only provide a collection and delivery service in and around Birmingham, but this idea had to be modified at the outset. There was no concern in London prepared to collect on the company's behalf, although there were four undertakings prepared to deliver any parcels taken in to them. These were, Carter, Paterson and its subsidiary, City & Suburban Carriers,

58

Above left: *One of the first batch of Red Arrow vans purchased in December 1933; they were 30cwt Bedfords with aluminium-panelled bodies by Wilsdon of Solihull and roller shutters at the rear; the recess on each side for posters (frequently changed) was standard on all RA vans.*

Left: *A 1937 addition to the Red Arrow fleet (another Bedford) for collection and delivery work in Bristol.*

Above: *A 1935 Commer to carry 2ton; besides the poster panels, all RA vans had an angle-iron step at rear to enable the driver to climb into the vehicle without taking the tailboard down unnecessarily.*

Pickfords and N. Francis & Son. Francis was independent but did not want to engage in long distance work; the others had all become railway owned. Hurst & Payne, therefore, hired an old Albion van to Red Arrow to start a collection service, while, for a time, deliveries were handed to Carter, Paterson. Eventually a small fleet was operated for both collection and delivery in the metropolitan area based on two depots, one at Malt Street, off Old Kent Road, and the other at Chiswick Common Road. The latter came to Red Arrow following the absorption of Speed Lines which served west Middlesex.

Another acquisition was that of Beech Transport of Coventry, working thence to Bristol in 1935. This not only gave Red Arrow a Coventry depot, but led to the establishment of a Bristol base and the stationing of two vans at the premises of All-British Carriers in Gloucester.

By 1939, Red Arrow had such extensive interworking arrangements that a reliable service could be given from the West Midlands to all parts of England and Wales (except the Lleyn Peninsula) and also to Southern and Central Scotland and up the north-east coast to Aberdeen and beyond. How this was done is set out in appendix B. It was the definite policy of the company to cater for cross-country routings. The purpose of acquiring Speed Lines was to tap the growing industries of west Middlesex and give a next day delivery in the Midlands, which could not be done by the railways or by other carriers who had first to cart goods into Central London. Similarly, Beech Transport was bought to enable a cross-country service to be given for small consignments of bacon and allied products from Wiltshire, which could not be remotely matched by rail or any other carrier.

The contacts made by Red Arrow brought many small carriers, who had hitherto worked in isolation, into touch with each other and led to a tremendous increase in interworking, to the great benefit of trade and industry. This, in turn, produced problems in regard to waybilling, methods of charging and claims. One of the greatest difficulties the pioneers of interworking had to contend with was the idea, then prevalent among traffic managers, that smalls could be

RED ARROW DELIVERIES

Express Carriers to all Principal Towns

MIDDLESEX AREA

UXBRIDGE

MIDDLESEX DEPOT:
40, Chiswick Common Rd., W.4
Telephone : Chiswick 5002

HEAD OFFICE:
BIRMINGHAM:
Waterloo Rd., S. Yardley. 25.
Telephone : ACOcks Green 1264

OTHER DEPOTS :

LONDON : Corner Wharf, Malt St., S.E.1.
Telephone : Bermondsey 1575

BRISTOL : Canning St., St. Paul's.
Telephone : Bristol 56935

GLOUCESTER : c/o All British Carriers Ltd.,
Merchants Rd.
Telephone : Gloucester 3877

LEICESTER : c/o Blands Ltd., Frog Island.
Telephone : Leicester 5127

COVENTRY : Minster Road.
Telephone : Coventry 2909

Above left: *Josiah Brevitt's carrying business at Willenhall, Staffs almost faded out during World War 1 and, when his grandson, Fred Rissbrook, joined him in 1920, he almost had to start from scratch and the first thing he did was to raise the money for a T-model Ford; this vehicle, restored to its original livery, was the sole exhibit on the Ford stand at the 1978 Motor Show.*

Left: *'Smalls' collected in the Black Country by Brevitt were taken to London for distribution by Allied Freight Services whose depot was in Long Lane, Bermondsey, and, besides returning with AFS smalls, Red Arrow surplus was carried to that company's depot at Yardley.*

Above: *When this map was published in 1938, the West Drayton area was just developing industrially and Heathrow Airport did not exist.*

carried at the low tonnage rates then prevailing for bulk loads as the result of intense and unregulated competition on the main routes.

I was an active member of Associated Road Operators, one of the constituents of the present Road Haulage Association, but found its meetings of little use to me as a parcels carrier. Moreover, ARO was not the only hauliers' association at that time. I felt that there ought to be some means of bringing together all parcels carriers to discuss their special problems and, in particular, to drive home to traders and to general hauliers that specialised service requires high rates.

I decided, as a first step, to get together all the carriers with whom Red Arrow was exchanging traffic. By this time (1937) a considerable number of other hauliers with no interchange arrangements was also leaving smalls at Red Arrow depots for delivery. Excluding these, 43 invitations were sent out to a meeting to be held at the Imperial Hotel, Birmingham on 28 September 1937. Thirty-four concerns accepted and all the others expressed interest, although unable to be represented. Delegates attended from as far away as Glasgow and Plymouth. Apart from the courtesies, the agenda was:

(a) Method of charging returned empties and allocation of such charges among the carriers concerned

(b) Notification of discrepancies

(c) Settlement of claims

(d) Rates between carriers; whether to be flat with minima, or scales similar to rail, or some other method

(e) Settlement of accounts between carriers, especially in regard to claims, CODs and carriage forwards

(f) Cost of giving proof of delivery by telegram or telephone

(g) The possibility of pooling with a view to quoting flat rates

(h) Holiday luggage

(i) The advisability of forming a permanent National Committee of Parcels Carriers

Although I knew everyone at the meeting, few of those who attended knew each other, so a special point was made of arranging the seating so that every one could be seen and identified from a table plan given to each delegate. Lunch was at the expense of Red Arrow and a visit was made to the company's depot.

By the time the last and really most important item on the agenda was reached, the idea of a permanent association for parcels carriers was enthusiastically received. How this came into existence and developed will be recounted later.

Chapter 7

When the Road & Rail Traffic Act came into force on 1 January 1934, it at once prevented any automatic increase in vehicle fleets, but the full effect was not felt until renewals of the first licences became due in 1936. A Ministry of Transport census for that year showed a total of 459,227 goods vehicles in use compared with 257,123 in 1926. The biggest increase was in vehicles under 3ton (it is not clear if this meant carrying capacity or unladen weight); these rose from 197,714 to 414,594. By contrast vehicles over 3tons showed a 24.9% decline from 59,409 to 44,633.

The railways owned large fleets of collection and delivery vehicles, 9,075 with 5,000 trailers plus 2,803 mechanical horses in 1936. In that year they also owned 13,125 horses and 25,217 horse-drawn vehicles, which were destined for eventual replacement.

The licensing authorities gave figures at 30 April 1936, 30 June 1937 and 30 June 1938 showing the following totals:

Number of Licence Holders

	April 1936	June 1937	June 1938
'A'	25,648	23,750	22,999
'A' contract	2,084	3,267	3,967
'B'	34,100	34,061	34,120
'C'	161,221	186,481	178,298
	223,053	247,559	239,384

Number of Vehicles Authorised and in Possession

	April 1936	June 1937	June 1938
'A'	85,337	83,626	83,749
'A' contract	5,156	7,475	9,467
'B'	52,809	53,775	54,906
'C'	316,714	362,380	365,025
	460,016	507,256	513,147

Below: Two Scammell 6-wheelers with Gardner engines supplied to Freeguard Bros shortly before they went into the Red & White group as All-British Carriers.

It will be seen that there was a decrease in both 'A' licensees and in the number of vehicles they owned, a large increase in contract 'A' licensees and vehicles; not much change in 'B' licences and a very large increase in 'C' licensed vehicles, particularly from 1936 to 1937. The recovery from the great slump in trade which was, by 1937, well under way, would have been reflected in an increase in 'A' licence operation but for the restrictive administration of the 1933 Act. Traders would not waste time going to court and submitting to rigorous cross-examination by railway counsel in support of a haulier's application for an extra ton or two on a licence if they had an amount of traffic to move which might justify the purchase of a vehicle. 'A' contract and 'C' licences were in effect, 'handed over the counter' and were often the easier way out.

Had the 1933 Act been administered in a more flexible way without the lawyers gaining a grip on the industry, there might have been far fewer 'A' contract and 'C'-licensed vehicles on the road. The Act, as it was interpreted, was self-defeating in its attempt to keep down the total number of commercial vehicles on the road and actually worked the other way.

It did, however, compel the professional hauliers to organise themselves better and, whenever possible to specialise, so that, by the outbreak of World War II, tramping in the style of the 1920s had almost died out. The specialists in household removals were less affected by the 1933 Act than most sections of the industry, as they had a long tradition of co-operation going back to the days of lift-vans which were carried over long distances by rail, this necessitating arrangements between the collecting remover and the firm making the delivery.

The Northamptonshire and Leicestershire specialists in loose boots and hosiery have been referred to in the previous chapter. A number of carriers in North London concentrated on new furniture and those at High Wycombe on chairs. Luton hats and their effect on van design have already been mentioned. Across the Pennines moved hundreds of lorries collecting raw wool or cotton from the ports and taking back finished goods. The bulky products of the Potteries called for a different method of operation and so the list could go on. By 1939 every trade and industry had experts in transporting its raw materials and finished products.

The trade associations only grew slowly and their membership was not a high proportion of the whole industry. They were concerned with politics and economics and not day-to-day operation, but there were many hauliers who felt that practical co-operation was vital to the industry. For the parcel

Below: *G. A. Renwick was a director of Scammell and when Fisher-Renwick changed from coastal shipping to long-distance road haulage, Scammells were an obvious choice; in the 1930s very fine specimens of both 8-wheelers and rigid sixes were produced, with Gardner diesel engines; Fisher Renwick's 8-wheelers, fitted with box-van bodies and claiming to give 'continuous service' were among the most familiar sights on the A5 and A45; it was F-R practice to name each vehicle.*

carriers with their regular services and clearly defined operating areas, cooperation was much easier to work out in practice than in the case of the tonnage hauliers.

When these at last got together their co-operation took two forms, either a loosely organised group or a limited company. E. B. Howes, who was the most vociferous advocate of the first form, organised the Saunders Group at Harpenden and this was typical. A third of the members, elected annually, formed an executive committee and one member was elected each year as controller. In effect each member subcontracted his surplus traffic to other members, but invoiced the customer himself, deducting 5% commission and passing the balance on to the firm which actually carried the goods. Each member agreed to open his books to other members, if they wished to check rates. The administrative charges of the group were met by a levy on the members.

Direct Motor Services (Sheffield) Ltd, formed in 1923, was an example of the other method. It never owned any vehicles. The manager placed traffic offered to the company to the best advantage of the members and profits were distributed in proportion to the shareholdings. Members wishing to sell had first to offer their shares to other members.

By contrast to these attempts to preserve the

independence of small operators while enabling them to avoid wasteful running, there was the growth of financial inter-linking between companies which, in their day-to-day operations, were self-governing. The expansion of Carter, Paterson and Pickfords has already been referred to. More spectacular was the growth of the Hanson & Holdsworth group, whose origins were mentioned in Chapter 4. I. W. Holdsworth Ltd bought J. W. North & Co Ltd of Bradford (1929), William Burrell Ltd of Littleborough (1931), J. Poulter & Sons Ltd of Bradford and Bradford-Leicester Transport Ltd of Sheffield (1934). The jointly-owned Holdsworth & Hanson (London) Ltd was formed in 1931 and separate companies in the joint name followed based on Leeds, Birmingham and Glasgow. The Leeds company took over Grimshaw & Evans, the Birmingham company bought the shares of J. W. Warrington Ltd and the Glasgow company took over the business of Wylie & Lockhead Ltd, the two latter in 1935. This led to a curious situation in Birmingham. Warrington's business had been the supply of vans to the Midland Red Parcels Department and, for a short time, to Red Arrow Deliveries. This work had ceased and both vans and premises were derelict, so Robert Hanson asked me to handle their work at the Red Arrow depot until they could get new premises built. When these were ready, Myers, managing director of Bradford-Leicester Transport, which had been working with Red Arrow from 1934, refused to transfer his collection and delivery work to the new associated company. (There was a similar situation with South Coast Carriers, the

Below: *Although this diagram was compiled in 1947, most of the companies shown were linked with Bristol Industries by 1939; many of them became part of British Road Services.*

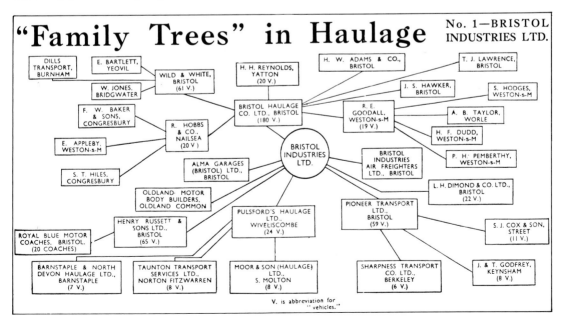

Carter, Paterson subsidiary, which had also been working with Red Arrow, and refused to transfer its deliveries to Pickfords when that company opened its new Birmingham depot.)

The largest acquisition of the Hanson & Holdsworth families was that of Oswald Tillotson Ltd of Burnley in 1935. This firm, which was a commercial vehicle dealer and bodybuilder, obtained control of Bouts in about 1930 and in December 1932 took over

Left: *After war service W. Donaldson Wright was appointed manager of the clearing house which Nottingham Chamber of Commerce started in 1919 to organise the growing demand for road transport; it was soon found that more was needed than merely an office, so a depot for transferring traffic was opened; eventually the Chamber decided that this was extraneous to its proper activities and the business was taken over by the Transport Services Group, who formed a company in Wright's name, which he managed until his retirement in 1948.*

Below: *E. W. Rudd, a London haulier, was among the earliest users of mechanical traction; the Scammell, shown here carrying a petrol-tank in 1925, must have been among the earliest built; Scammell started a factory for petrol-driven chassis at Watford in 1924.*

Mac Carriers Ltd whose origins have also been described earlier. Other acquisitions were W. V. Greenwood Ltd of Burnley, Same Day Delivery also of Burnley, City Express Motors Ltd of Bradford and R. V. Morris of Norwich. Tillotson's biggest acquisition was Ryburn United Transport Ltd of Bradford with a fleet of about 100. The effect of all this was, that half way through the 1930s, Oliver and Charles Holdsworth and Robert and Donald Hanson

Right: To the casual observer it may seem surprising that in the climate of Yorkshire and Lancashire there should be such a high proportion of lorries rather than vans carrying textiles; this is the reason — so many warehouses with delivery required on an upper floor; the vehicle is an AEC Mandator.

Below: Here is another Albion built for a 10-ton load but this time with the additional axle at the rear to give a longer wheelbase; the Albion Motor Car Company, founded at Scotstoun in 1901, had a great reputation for reliability, but was very conservative; it stuck to chain-drive long after other major builders and it was reluctant to change from petrol to diesel; this vehicle was photographed in 1934.

Above: *ERF was the result of a family rumpus when Edwin R. Foden set up his own business, starting production in 1933; lorries and tractors with the name are more common than vans, but Scott, who was a parcel carrier must have ordered this 7¼-tonner with Gardner engine and 5-speed gearbox for trunk service; it is shown with wartime headlamp masks.*

Above right: *Several makers in the 1930s favoured twin-steering 6-wheelers for 10ton loads, as Foden did in this example with a Gardner 5LW engine; this van (like Premier's on another page) has flaps above the cab at the front to accommodate items of exceptional length.*

controlled about 450 goods vehicles, apart from their passenger interests and other activities such as the fuel distribution company, Trent Oil Products.

A remarkable development was Transport Services Ltd, which Claud Barrington evolved from the clearing house of Carey, Davies and Thomas. He secured the interest of Harley Drayton, a prominent financier who had started his career as assistant to J. Austin, a director of the British Electric Traction group, and Transport Services was floated in 1936 as a public company with Philip Dunn as chairman and Barrington as managing director. Other directors were S. Royle and E. C. Simon. Under the main company there were eventually 26 subsidiary companies. The main strength of the group was in general haulage. London-based firms acquired were General Roadways Ltd, Kneller & Chandler Ltd, North-Western Transport Services Ltd.

General haulage firms acquired in the provinces were Kinder's Transport Ltd and Quinceys Ltd, both of Leicester; Hulton Motor Co Ltd and A. H. Barlow (Transport) Ltd of Manchester; Davies & Brownlow Ltd (St Helens); J. Blaney Ltd and Northumbrian Transport Service Ltd both of Gateshead; NWTS (Hull) Ltd; West Midland Roadways Ltd (Burton-on-Trent); Southern Transport Co Ltd (Brighton); Edwards & Sons (Transport) Ltd (Folkestone); Fred Rees (Neyland) Ltd; John Ford (Pembroke) Ltd;

Cullingford & Collett Ltd (Yoxford); Sudbury (Suffolk) Transport Service Ltd (Ipswich). Four London firms were mainly concerned with the provision trade or with market deliveries; these were Bert Whiting Ltd, W. Bradbrook & Son Ltd, S. J. Megenis Ltd and Henry Bayes Ltd.

The Nottingham Chamber of Commerce Transport Clearing House was taken over and as Donaldson Wright Ltd became a fleet owner parcel carrier (W. Donaldson Wright was the manager). Other express carriers acquired were Gamman & Dicker Ltd of Chatham, who were also barge owners until the mid-1930s and Child & Pullen Ltd of Ipswich. C. D. & T. (Contracts) Ltd, as its name implies, supplied vehicles on regular contract to ancillary users.

In the bus world, the Watts family of Lydney and the Bowns of Brynmawr built up a considerable business in the 1920s, which, under the name of Red & White United Transport, first covered a large part of Monmouthshire, Herefordshire and Gloucestershire and then spread, through subsidiaries, across South Wales and into the South Midlands.

With growing stability in haulage after the 1933 Act, the Watts group decided to invest in that section of the industry and acquired control of Freeguard Bros of Newport, who ran regular services thence to London and Birmingham. When the group bought Blue Belle, the London coach operators, part of the Clapham Road coach station was let to All-British Carriers (as the Freeguard business had been renamed) as its London depot. The group also developed Bulwark Transport, specialising in the carriage of bulk liquids.

London & Southern Counties Transport has been mentioned in an earlier chapter. In 1938 or 1939 this was amalgamated with H. Pye & Son as Pye and Counties and Watts took a financial interest in this also. Pye had specialised in contract hire, with its main base at Melksham, but the head office of the new company was at Southampton Way, Camberwell. J. F. E. Pye, son of H. Pye, was managing director and A. Packham, who had been assistant to R. W. Sewill at London & Southern became assistant managing director. Sewill was on the board (although by then he was a full-time official of Associated Road Operators). J. H. Watts was chairman and other directors were Gerald Nowell (a Red & White man), H. Pye and A. J. Watts.

Bristol Industries Ltd, one of the many concerns in which the Wills family have had an interest, also began building up a large haulage group, while maintaining the identities of the acquired companies. Bristol Haulage Co Ltd was a tonnage carrier, but the group included Henry Russett & Sons Ltd, Wild and White and Pioneer Transport Ltd which were parcels carriers and L. H. Dimond & Co Ltd which besides general carrying was a furniture remover.

The most ambitious attempt at combination was prompted by Reginald Hindley, an accountant of Ashton-under-Lyne, who became active in Associated Road Operators. He interested a wellknown financier, Szarvasy, in the idea of a nationwide group covering all aspects of haulage. During 1938-9, Hindley and Szarvasy toured the country, inspecting hauliers' premises and discussing their proposals with leading operators. For the most part the response was not enthusiastic, but they did succeed in forming Hauliers Ltd which was incorporated on 24 August 1939 with an authorised capital of £200,000 divided into 50,000 6% preference shares of £1 each and 150,000 ordinary shares of £1 each.

Even for those days this did not seem a very large capital for an organisation with such great aims, especially as it was proposed to acquire businesses simply by the issue of shares in Hauliers. In fact, the group started as an amalgamation of Edward Box & Co Ltd and Beresford Caddy and Pemberton Ltd. These were two very different concerns. BCP (as it was generally known) was itself an amalgamation, with the Beresford constituent going back to 1865. It was based on Tunstall and, in addition to carrying the products of the Potteries to the ports of Liverpool, Manchester and London, had a smalls business operating between Manchester, Tunstall and Birmingham. It was one of the firms that worked with Red Arrow. Edward Box, by contrast, relied for the bulk of its business on heavy movements, particularly of abnormal individual loads, and because of the greater value of its rolling stock compared with that of BCP, it was allotted preference shares in the amalgamation.

The first board of Hauliers reflected the relationship of the two companies. H. E. Crawfurd, then president of ARO, was chairman and the other directors were Ralph Donaldson-Hudson and his son John, chairman and managing director respectively of Box, and J. W. Beresford, chairman of B. C. P. Hindley was co-ordinating officer, working from his office in Corn Exchange Buildings, Manchester, and his firm the auditors. J. Broadley was secretary and Mawby, Barrie and Letts of London, who specialised in haulage cases, were the solicitors. The registered office was at 426, Bush House (Crawfurd's office). England and Wales were divided into five zones and a subsidiary company was formed for each, with the

Above: Allan Simpson dealt with parcels and 'smalls' and one wonders why in 1933, it chose Leyland Cubs with six wheels, instead of the 4-wheeled version, unless it was to get a longer body to accommodate the bulkiness of parcels; what, too, was the reason for the fixed head boards and roll-back tilts?

intention of giving any absorbed undertakings some measure of local control.

In its first year Hauliers absorbed Walker Bros (Brighouse) Ltd, Ware Transport Co Ltd of Peterborough, Airlandwater Transport Co Ltd of Bishop's Stortford, Butterwick Transport Ltd of Leeds, C. F. Denning (Transport) Ltd of Epping and Newcastle Transport & Trading Co Ltd of Stockton-on-Tees, but the war stopped further expansion.

In the United Kingdom the most spectacular move to establish an orderly system co-ordinating road and rail was the passing of the Road & Railway Transport Act (Northern Ireland), 1935 which established the Northern Ireland Road Transport Board. This was empowered to take over all the 66 passenger undertakings in the Six Counties, except that of Belfast Corporation, and also all road goods transport plying for hire or reward, except vehicles engaged in furniture removals or the carriage of horses. Vehicles on purely local work in Belfast and Londonderry were also excluded. The Board was in difficulties from its start on 1 October 1935. There was no carrier or operator licensing in force in Northern Ireland, so that it was difficult to determine which goods businesses should be acquired. Even when this was ascertained the value of the businesses was usually a matter of guesswork. As the Board's first report said:

'There were a large number of cases in which there was either no records at all, or records of a very partial and incomplete character. In many cases the accounts consisted entirely of estimates'.

The Board started, quite logically, by taking over the road transport undertakings of the three railways in its area, plus the two largest bus companies which were also the only ones with anything like an efficient organisation. When it went on to the smaller bus operators it found, to quote again from its first report, that:

'In most cases the fares were on no settled basis at all, and many operators were accustomed to depart from their ordinary fare lists in favour of particular individuals. On many routes it was almost impossible to ascertain, with any degree of certainty, what fares were charged, as frequently the conductors exercised their own discretion and did not adhere to any fare list'.

Its country operations were badly affected by competition from vehicles seating six persons in addition to the driver.

When the Board systematically began to take over haulage concerns, it soon found that, when it thought it had acquired a monopoly in a particular area, hauliers from areas which had not been tackled, moved in and cut the Board's rates. It also found that in many cases, owners who had been paid for their businesses used the money to start up again in some guise or other. Notice by the Board that it was going to acquire businesses in a certain area usually led to manufacturers and traders buying their own vehicles in case the Board put up rates. Thus it was alleged (although without proof), at a public enquiry in May 1938, that there were 2,000 more lorries on the road than when the Board took over, despite the Board's having scrapped a large percentage of its acquired vehicles.

In the two years ending September 1937, the Board took over 692 buses and 1,417 lorries. Of the goods vehicles, 1,158, belonging to 984 different owners were acquired in the year 1936-7. These figures indicate the magnitude of the task the Board had in assimilating the private undertakings. Undoubtedly there were far too many vehicles on the road for the needs of the area and this is reflected in the decreased size of the Board's fleet which by 1940 was down to 493 buses and 661 lorries.

Payment for the acquired undertakings was by the issue of stock bearing interest at 4% and redeemable between 1970 and 1995 (A stock) or after 1970, at the Board's discretion (B stock), and by cash. The railway-owned undertakings and the Belfast Omnibus and Catherwood businesses were paid for entirely by stock. Nearly all the other owners were given cash but a few received payment partly in stock and partly in cash. The Board was landed with hundreds of decrepit vehicles and a total far in excess of its needs so that in its first three years it had to provide £109,000 for abnormal depreciation over and in addition to normal depreciation.

The Act establishing the Board provided for a Joint Committee with the railways and imposed on both parties the obligation to devise a pool of net receipts. The pool was to be worked on the basis of a standard year. In the case of the railways this was to be calculated by taking half the net receipts for 1924 and 1932 and adding them together. For the Board the standard was to be the net receipts of the acquired undertakings for 1932. The railways were to put into the pool the whole of the receipts 'accruing from the conveyance of passengers and merchandise in Northern Ireland, excluding station terminal charges' and the Board was to put in the whole of its net receipts. Why the railways were to exclude 'station terminal charges' is not clear. The Board's task in calculating reliable figures for 1932 was hopeless, as may be imagined from what has already been said about the acquired undertakings, and, in fact, receipts never were pooled.

It was not until the summer of 1937, that the Board was really in a position to organise its freight business on efficient lines. It not only had difficulty in the financial aspects of the hundreds of takeovers but also the physical problem of where to put the vehicles. Outside Belfast in the first three years it had to build 20 new depots. In Belfast itself it started by using premises belonging to the London, Midland & Scottish Railway as a parcels depot, but these proved to be unsuitable and other premises belonging to the Great Northern Railway (Ireland) in Grosvenor Road were acquired and adapted. It also started its own bodybuilding department in Duncrue Street, Belfast.

In the year ending 30 September 1939, the Board showed every sign of really getting on to its feet. There was an overall profit on operation of £7,693 as against a loss the previous year of £76,206. The freight side, despite some four months of slump, reduced its deficit, which was £69,032 in 1937-8, to £37,524. The figure of £7,693 was reached after allowing £125,328 for depreciation. During the year the Board paid out £97,131 in interest, so that the accumulated debit balance in the Board's accounts from its inception came to £521,935 of which £323,964 was interest paid. By this time 1,206 undertakings (goods and passenger) had been acquired.

It is outside the scope of this book to describe the Board's activities during the war but, as it was merged into the new Ulster Transport Authority on 30 September 1948, a summary of its achievements is appropriate. A small but interesting point is that in September, 1939, the Board had 18 horses and 46 horse-drawn vehicles and at the end of its existence still had nine horses and 19 vehicles. The horses had been of great use in saving fuel. The Board had to hire extensively to augment its fleet during World War II but it ended its life actually owning 945 buses and 981 goods vehicles compared with 505 and 223 in 1935. In its life of 13 years, annual traffic receipts rose from £676,731 to £3,820,633; vehicle mileage from 15 to 47 million and staff from about 3,000 to 7,124.

After 1940, the Board was able to clear off the losses of the earlier years and the net result of its 13 years' activities was a credit balance of £194,558, after providing for depreciation and renewals and paying all interest, redemption and taxation charges. The undertaking was grossly over-capitalised to start with by having to buy businesses on the basis of 10 years' profits instead of about three as would have been ordinary commercial practice, and it was saddled with hundreds of useless vehicles. In the year 1939-40, the A and B stockholders were bought out by the Northern Ireland Government but the Board had to make an annual payment to the Ministry of Finance towards the cost of redemption.

There can be littler doubt that the Board was hamstrung by the attitude of the railway managements and by local politics. It should have been obvious, even

Below: All-British Carriers was the name assumed by Freeguard Bros after the company was taken into John Watt's Red & White group; Red & White while best known as bus operators also obtained control of Pye and Counties, itself a fusion of H. Pye & Son and London & Southern Counties; All-British had a London depot at the Clapham Road Coach Station.

Right: An AEC Mammoth Major in service in Cornwall.

at that time, that Ulster could not support a railway system as extensive as it was, but the railways were determined to maintain the dominant position, which, in fact, they had already lost. The Board and its officers were victims of continual sniping, although the 1938 public enquiry ended in finding little substance in the large volume of complaints about services and charges. This was only one of several enquiries during the life of the Board, seemingly inspired for the most part by hatred of the idea of public ownership. The Board and its officers had to waste a formidable amount of their time in combatting the allegations against their efficiency. The Board's chairman was D. L. Clarke and its first general manager James McCrea. He had to retire because of ill-health in February 1937 and was succeeded by Albert Morrison. Other principal officers were W. E. MacVe, deputy general manager, James Courtney, chief engineer and J. A. Clarke, secretary. W. E. MacVe, who had been transport manager of the Bleachers' Association, left in 1944 to become North Western Regional Transport Commissioner. The Board's offices were at Queen's Buildings, Royal Avenue, Belfast.

Chapter 8

In 1919 there were a number of local associations of cart and (horse-drawn) lorry owners, some of whose members also owned motors and, probably in 1921 (the exact date has not been found), 15 of these came together to form the National Road Transport Employers' Federation. The largest constituents were based on London, Bristol, Liverpool, Sheffield and Glasgow. R. P. Bailey, the secretary of the London & Home Counties Haulage Contractors' Association, undertook also the secretaryship of the Federation. His office was at 17 Water Lane, EC. Even as late as 1930 large numbers of horse vehicles were still employed by Federation members, particularly in dock and market work.

An organisation with undivided loyalty to mechanical traction was the Commercial Motor Users' Association, founded in 1906 by members of the Royal Automobile Club, with Frederick George Bristow as general secretary. Bristow had the distinction of holding this office as long as the CMUA existed, ie until 1945. There was a separate CMUA for Scotland. Although it included many haulier members, the CMUA was predominantly an ancillary users'

organisation. This is not surprising because, at the end of 1929, it was estimated, in evidence before the Royal Commission on Transport, that of the 360,000 goods-carrying vehicles in Great Britain, some 288,000 were employed by traders solely for their own use, but it deterred most of the newcomers to haulage from joining the CMUA even when they were men who saw the need for an association. The great majority did not, unfortunately, so that the Royal Commission had no source from which to obtain evidence on their behalf.

Below: Laurie Gupwell, who, with his brother, inherited a family shop-fitting business in Birmingham expanded into general haulage and the firm's lorries were a familiar sight on the London and Liverpool roads; this Octopus was in service in 1937.

Right: Whitbreds was using this Dennis 3½-tonner in the Isle of Wight in 1932; at its London headquarters in 1938 it had six Thornycroft Nippys, with hardwood sided bodies by Marshalls of Cambridge, who also supplied the cabs.

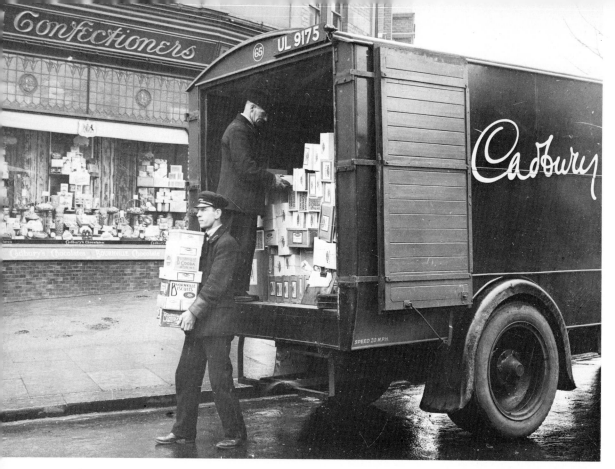

There was also a specialist organisation, the National Association of Furniture Removers & Warehousemen, many of whose members continued to use horses for most of the 1920s. This association was early in developing co-operation among its members for part-loads. It also enabled members to use lift-vans which could be sent by rail to distant points and there be delivered by other members.

The NRTEF, CMUA and SCMUA were members of the Standing Joint Committee of Mechanical Road Transport Associations mentioned earlier in connection with the Royal Commission. The SJC also included the private motorists organisations and, apparently, came into existence originally as a group to keep motor taxation down. There was also a Motor Transport Employers' Federation (not to be confused with the NRTEF), of which little is now known. It seems to have been a CMUA offshoot, designed to keep the association itself out of wage negotiations. Bristow of the CMUA was secretary of this body as well as of the SJC.

In the winter of 1929-30, G. Mackenzie Junner, editor of *The Commercial Motor* commissioned E. B. Hutchinson to travel round the country and write

some articles about the haulage industry. Hutchinson, as already mentioned, was not a haulier but a highly successful busman, the creator of United Autombile Services, which he sold to the railways in 1929. He was astonished at the lack of organisation among hauliers and his report prompted Junner to invite some prominent members of the industry to a lunch at Pagani's Restaurant in Great Portland Street on 29 April 1930.

The occasion was recalled 36 years later in a *The Commercial Motor* article by J. A. M. Bright who was one of those present, and at that time joint managing director of Southern Roadways Ltd of Poole. He later ran Onward Transport of Selby. The others at the lunch besides Junner and Hutchinson were C. Adams, C. R. P. Dalgleish (who ran a family business in Nottingham), W. Donaldson Wright (Nottingham Chamber of Commerce), M. W. Dring (Northern Motor Utilities Ltd, York), W. F. French (United Service Transport Ltd, London), L. W. Gupwell (A. J. Gupwell Ltd, Birmingham), Sir Maxwell Hicks (McNamara & Co Ltd), K. S. Kneller (Kneller & Chandler Ltd, London), E. C. Marston (MRS Ltd), H. Scott Hall (who wrote on rates and costs in *The*

Commercial Motor over the initials 'STR'), H. Turner and W. A. Vacher (assistant editor of *The Commercial Motor*).

It was agreed to form a Long Distance Road Haulage Committee of Enquiry and when this committee met for the first time on 6 May at the offices of Sir Maxwell Hicks (12 Grosvenor Gardens) he was elected chairman and E. B. Hutchinson's offer to act as honorary secretary was accepted. P. R. Turner, managing director of Thomas Allen Ltd and a vice-chairman of the National Road Transport Employers' Federation was co-opted to the committee.

From this committee developed the Long Distance Road Haulage Association, which it was decided to form at a meeting held at Winchester House, London in January 1931. Those present at the meeting authorised the existing committee to carry on as the committee of the new association with the substitution of J. S. Nicholl of McNamara for Sir Maxwell Hicks and the addition of Roger W. Sewill of London & Southern Counties Transport. The committee then adjourned to the Victoria Hotel, Northumberland Avenue, where E. C. Marston was elected chairman. E. B. Hutchinson agreed to continue as honorary secretary working from his office in Leeds, but the new association grew so rapidly during the year that it was able to engage a wholetime secretary, J. M. Mackenzie, who started work on 1 January 1932 from an office in Dudley House, Southampton Street, Covent Garden.

Also in 1931, a Short Distance Hauliers' Alliance came into existence, the moving spirit being Frank F. Fowler, who was engaged mainly in tipping work in south-west London. The two new bodies eventually amalgamated under the simple and adequate name of the Road Haulage Association. Its advent was not welcomed by the CMUA or NRTEF, but it undoubtedly appealed to the large number of hauliers with few vehicles in a way the older bodies did not.

Marston continued as chairman and Nicholl and Sewill as vice-chairmen of the combined body. Other members of the National Council were F. F. Fowler, E. G. Gordon-Poggi, L. W. Gupwell, E. B. Hutchinson, H. Janes, J. W. Jones, S. F. Kneller, E. R. Marston, J. F. E. Pye, D. Richardson, L. J. Rix, S. R. Saunders, R. B. Stockdale, E. C. Thomas, A. Todd, T. Topham, C. E. Treadwell, W. Donaldson Wright and O. G. Wynn.

In addition to the old local cartage associations which came together in the NRTF, there were, in the

1920s, a number of local bodies which seem to have been composed originally of horse-vehicle owners who were gradually converting to motors and were undecided whether to be pasenger or goods operators. Twenty-two of these affiliated themselves to The Motor Hirers' & Coach Services Association, of which F. A. Walker was secretary. Successful negotiations in 1935 resulted in the amalgamation of this body with the RHA.

A new organisation was then registered on 12 July 1935 with the title of Associated Road Operators. It was registered as a company limited by guarantee without share capital. The first subscribers were J. S. Nicholl, A. L. Guilmant, L. W. Gupwell, J. F. E. Pye and F. F. Fowler from the R. H. A. and F. A. Flin and R. W. Birch (both coach operators) from the Motor Hirers. Offices were taken at Grand Buildings, Trafalgar Square and Major J. B. Elliott was elected first chairman of the national council. R. W. Sewill, while remaining a director of London & Southern Counties, ceased to be joint managing director and was appointed national director of ARO. Clifford H. Gale was engaged as general secretary and F. A. Walker was given special responsibility as secretary of the passenger vehicle section.

In 1936, negotiations took place between ARO and CMUA with a view to amalgamation. When these broke down, certain members of both bodies in some areas (of which Birmingham was one) decided to take independent action and to amalgamate locally. The net result seems to have been, in effect, a small secession from ARO to the CMUA.

The position of the employers' associations in 1937 was thus an illogical one. The furniture removers had their own specialist organisation, there were old local associations mostly under the umbrella of the NRTEF, plus ARO, the CMUA and the SCMUA which were mixed bodies not solely concerned with professional hauliers. Reference has already been made to the meeting of parcels carriers which I called in Birmingham on 28 September 1937. The proposal to form a permanent National Committee of Parcels Carriers was accepted by those present and David Richardson of Gamman & Dicker Ltd, Chatham, offered to call a meeting to start the committee during the forthcoming Commercial Motor Show at Earl's Court.

This meeting was held on 8 November 1937. Twenty-nine operators were represented varying in size from owners of hundreds of vehicles to one owning three. All became foundation members as did seven others who were unable to attend. It was appropriate that E. B. Hutchinson was present as an interested observer. When the meeting opened I was elected chairman and at once moved a motion, which, on being carried unanimously, established a National

Above: *Lyons used Karrier Cob Juniors to draw semi-trailers for side loading; the small bogie which came down to support the van as the tractor drew away can be seen under the van on the left.*

Conference of Parcels Carriers. A central executive committee was then nominated.

When this met in Birmingham on 2 December 1937, it had to face a disturbing development. The railway-controlled companies, acting on instructions from above, declined to proceed with membership of the conference and were not represented.

At that time, the campaign of the railways for a 'Square Deal' was being prepared and was, in fact, launched in 1938, as described in Chapter 11. The Ministry of Transport was under pressure from the then powerful railway interests to secure more 'order' in road transport than had, up to then, resulted from the Road and Rail Traffic Act, 1933. The Transport Advisory Council (see Chapter 9) which had given lengthy consideration to the subject of coordination, had said that the fixation of road rates (preferably by the industry itself) was a first essential.

The threat of the 'square deal' prompted a joint meeting on 27 January 1938 of the ARO, the CMUA, the NAFWR and the NRTEF. These agreed to form a liaison committee under the aegis of the British Road Federation and were subsequently joined by the SCMUA.

It was made clear to a deputation from the Liaison Committee which went to the Ministry of Transport on 23 February 1938 that before the government would introduce a bill for the statutory control of road rates it expected the industry to work out a rates structure itself. The Committee, therefore, decided to begin by formulating standard conditions of carriage.

In these circumstances, the independent parcels carriers were most anxious that future smalls rates shoud not be decided solely on the experience of the railway-associated concerns. The Executive, therefore, authorised David Richardson and me to do all in our power to bring in the railway-associated concerns.

One reason for their abstention became apparent very soon after. Among the constituents of the NRTEF was the London Cartage Association, to which Carter. Paterson and Pickfords had belonged for many years. On 23 February 1938, the secretary of the Federation (R. P. Bailey) wrote to all the principal smalls carriers suggesting a conference of those engaged in 'collection and delivery work'.

This appeared to be duplicating what the Parcels Conference had set out to do, so I at once contacted Mr Bailey. Meetings were held at his office on 7 March and 8 April and a very satisfactory modus vivendi was reached, and confirmed by the Parcels Carriers' Executive on 22 April 1938. The arrangement was that G. W. Quick Smith, then assistant secretary of the Federation, should also become the part-time secretary of the Parcels Conference, replacing R. B. Brittain of National Parcels (later renamed Essex Carriers Ltd) who had acted as honorary secretary.

With this agreement in force, James Paterson of Carter, Paterson and W. J. Elliott, general manager of Pickfords were able to persuade their overlords to allow the railway-owned companies to join the conference, where they did excellent work. Paterson became president of the Conference (1938-42) and was succeeded by Elliott. It was on the suggestion of N. D. Fawkner, general manager of Carter, Paterson, that when the Conference executive met on 13 July 1938 to approve a formal constitution and rules, the name was changed to the National Conference of Express Carriers. He was also appointed chairman of a sub-committee which had been appointed on 14 March 1938 to evolve a standard set of conditions of carriage, as an important prelude to any attempt at classification. Even among express carriers at this time, the great majority had no standard conditions and it would probably be true to say that the very idea was unknown to general hauliers, who were operating with no legal protection whatever against false and fraudulent claims.

The meeting of 22 April, which had appointed Quick Smith as secretary also took the important step of asking for representation on the BRF's Liaison Committee on Rates, which had also appointed a sub-committee on conditions of carriage. When the parcels men joined this committee they at once found themselves in disagreement with the general hauliers on the question of liability, which, for smalls carriers must be related to the value of the individual package as against the value of a load. Other complications occurred at this time which are set out in Chapter 11.

Above: Although drawbar-trailers are now not often seen they were widely used up to 1939, although legislation compelled the carrying of an 'attendant' long after the need for one had passed (originally the trailer brakes were controlled by a cable operated by a wheel in the driver's cab); Timothy White, having widespread branches probably found it convenient to leave a trailer to be off-loaded while the motive-power went somewhere else; this AEC van, judging by the sheet at the back had both rear and side-loading facilities.

It is unlikely that the date 27 August 1910, will ever be quoted in the ordinary history books, but a decision made that day was ultimately to have a considerable effect on the social and political life of this country and, indeed, of Europe. A 29-year old Somerset man, earning his living by selling mineral waters from door to door in Bristol, decided to join the Dock, Wharf, Riverside & General Workers' Union. His name was Ernest Bevin.

He immediately started a campaign to enrol the Bristol carters into a separate branch of the union and became branch chairman. The following year he took the risk of giving up his job, to join the staff of the union as an organiser with a wage of £2 a week.

At this time there were a number of local organisations for carters, who were, of course, with very few exceptions, horse-drivers. Scotland will be referred to later. In England such bodies existed in Liverpool, Manchester and Leeds. Where there was no separate association for carters some were organised, as at Bristol, by the general workers unions.

In 1910, on the initiative of the Dockers' Union, a National Transport Workers' Federation was formed under the leadership of Ben Tillett. It was a loose grouping of 30 unions concerned with port work and included several of those concerned with road transport workers. Bevin rose rapidly in the councils of his union and in 1916 he was nominated as its representative on the executive of the federation. In August 1918, he was chairman of a conference of 17 unions, having members among carters and motormen, which met in Salford to plan a campaign to secure a uniform increase over prewar wages. In 1919-20 he became nationally known as 'the dockers' KC' through his powerful advocacy before an industrial court and he was the obvious leader of the workers' side when a Joint Industrial Council for Road Transport was formed, but an attempt in 1920 to secure a national minimum wage of £4 7s a week for lorry drivers failed. There was insufficient organisation among the men to ensure the success of a strike and the only result was that the JIC came to an end.

But the same year was, nevertheless, one of triumph for Bevin as he successfully conducted negotiations for the formation of the Transport & General Workers' Union, which came into existence on 1 January 1921.

Its great feature was the semi-autonomy of the constituent trade groups. It was this feature that induced unions in a wide variety of trade to join together and enabled Bevin to bring in as from 1 January 1922, unions representing vehicle workers (ie bus and tram men) and carters.

The TGWU grew in total strength throughout the 1920s and 1930s but made hardly any progress among the new race of long-distance drivers. Right up to 1939, its road transport (goods) membership was almost entirely employed in dock and local delivery work.

An organisation of drivers which has survived as a body completely independent of the TGWU is the United Road Transport Union, with its head office in Manchester, where it was started on 1 February 1890. It was then called the United Carters' Association. The following year 'of England' was added to the title. Another change in 1912 made it the United Carters' & Motormen's Association of England; then, in 1926, it became the United Road Transport Workers' Association of England. The present title dates from 1964. At the period of which I am writing, membership of the United was concentrated in the north of England. Its secretary was J. C. Francis.

Left: Could this Tilling-Stevens loading hops in 1926 have been an old bus chassis although that was the year in which T-S started turning out more conventional chassis with clutch and friction-drive?; the petrol-electric system, in which the petrol engine drove a dynamo the current from which activated an electric motor was devised to ease the changeover from horse-traction to mechanical, since it has no gears.

Jackson Moore, the present general secretary of the United, has given me the copy I reproduce of a leaflet put out by his union in 1923, which shows how the unions were fighting to stop wages going down. The phraseology about the cost of living relates to percentage above pre-war. The leaflet also brings out the importance at that time of steam and horse-traction. The distinction between the Ford and other petrol-driven vehicles is interesting.

The story of labour relations in Scottish commercial transport is a bitter one, with the employees' organisations often fighting among themselves as well as contending with the employers. The story is told in detail in Angela Tuckett's *The Scottish Carter*, but the reader must be warned that when Miss Tuckett strays away from the minutes of the workers' organisations, her version of events does not always agree with my personal knowledge of them. She traces the Scottish Horse & Motormen's Association, which has lasted to the present day, to the Scottish Carters' Association which was founded on 29 October 1898 and changed its name on 16 August 1908, but there were earlier associations. There were also some entirely local ones. The SH & MA refused to join the National Transport Workers' Federation because it was controlled from London and from the time Bevin made the TGWU a power, there was much fighting in Scotland for membership. Some local bodies went in with Bevin; others refused.

A general strike of carters on Clydeside in January 1919 secured a 48-hour week but from then on the employees were fighting a losing battle and this was reflected in the membership strength of the Horse & Motormen. The 14,767 members of 1919 had fallen to 7,596 by 1932 (less than in 1912).

An Industrial ('Whitley') Council for Road Transport in Scotland was set up in October 1919 with the Scottish Carting Contractors' & Horse Owners' Federation on one side and the SH & MA on the other. It fixed the minimum wage for 48 hours for drivers of steam wagons at £4 5s and for second men at £4. Drivers of petrol motors were to get £3 10s. In 1920 wages began to fall and in 1921 the Association was forced to accept an agreement which provided for a revision of wages every three months. Wages were to

be reduced by 3s a week immediately and a further 2s when the cost of living fell to 130 points above pre-war; thereafter there was to be a reduction or an increase of one shilling for each five points variation. Between April 1921 and August 1923, the men had nine reductions totalling £1 0s 6d. A carter's wage was then supposed to be £2 10s a motor driver's £2 19s and a steam driver's £3 9s, but it was said that many received less. As late as 1931, the Association was fighting for a minimum wage for carters of £2 10s.

During the 1920s and 1930s, the gradual motorisation of the railway companies' collection and delivery fleets, with the railways in some cases taking over themselves from contractors led to numerous conflicts between the association and the National Union of Railwaymen. The frequent friction with the TGWU was much reduced by an agreement in 1927 which divided the areas for recruitment among the two bodies, but there was never any love lost between them and the Association's members did not wholly or whole-heartedly join the General Strike of 1926 and there were instances of violence when pickets attempted to stop association members from delivering to or from employers to whom the association had given permits. These seem to have been mainly concerned with food-stuffs, coal and other essentials. Because it was outside the National Transport Workers' Federation, the association was not represented on the Joint Transport Committee which directed the strike. Internal squabbles culminated in the dismissal in 1936 of Hugh Lyon, who had been secretary for 34 years and his replacement by Robert Taylor.

On the employers' side in addition to the Scottish Commercial Motor Users' Association, there were during this period, the Scottish Horse & Motor Contractors' Federation (secretary T. Worsley) and the Scottish Carriers' & Hauliers' Association.

The Road Traffic Act, 1930, section 93, gave the unions a statutory right to intervene by appeal to the Industrial Court in cases where it appeared that wages were not being paid to public service vehicle drivers consistent with any current resolution of the House of Commons applicable to wages paid by contractors to the government. Section 32 of the Road & Rail Traffic Act, 1933 extended this provision to holders of 'A' and 'B' licences and included decisions of joint industrial councils and conciliation boards as yardsticks. It also referred to 'an agreement between organisations representative of employers and workpeople' as one of the criteria should a case go to an industrial court.

The important point about this section is that it became a condition of every 'A' and 'B' licence which it was an offence to break; but what, in practice, were the supposed standards worth? The fragmentation of the employers' organisations and relatively small membership both of these and of the appropriate union group made a national agreement hardly practicable. In this situation the Minister of Labour consulted two employers' representatives (W. Edwards and J. S. Nicholl) and two union officials (E. Bevin and A. N. Denaro). On their recommendation, a National Joint Conciliation Board for the Road Motor Transport Industry (Goods) was set up in March 1934 under the chairmanship of Sir Richard Redmayne, a former Chief Inspector of Mines. The Board consisted of 30 members, 15 from each side. The Employers' representatives were five each from the NRTEF, the Motor Transport Employers' Federation and the Road Haulage Association (later, as already related, merged into ARO). The union side had 10 members from the TGWU, two from the United Road Transport Workers' Association of England, two from the Liverpool & District Carters' & Motormen's Union and one from the National Union of General & Municipal Workers. W. Edwards headed the employers' side and Bevin the trade union side. The joint secretaries were R. P. Bailey of the NRTEF and J. E. Corrin, national secretary of the TGWU's Road Transport Commercial Group. Provision was made for area boards also.

In December, 1934, the Board published its decisions on working conditions and wages which were to come into force throughout England and Wales on 1 January 1935. A 48-hour week (Monday to Saturday) was to be guaranteed on an accumulative basis, exclusive of mealtimes. There were provisions for overtime and for minimum payments when a regular man was called in and for casual employees. All Sunday work was to be at time-and-a-half within a minimum payment for four hours, except that a regular man could be employed for $2\frac{1}{2}$ hours solely to attend to his vehicle. A man away from home and off duty overnight was to paid 5s with an extra 2s 6d if the time exceeded 12 hours or a total of 10s if the time exceeded 18 hours. In addition to public holidays, every man with at least one year's service was to have a week's paid leave annually.

For the payment of wages drivers were divided into: (1) those employed in London and the Metropolitan Area; (2) those on trunk and long-distance work; (3) all others. Youths and attendants formed a fourth

Below: New in 1925, a Mann undertype steamer with an unladen weight of six tons built to carry six tons.

Right: The peculiarities of dock working have often been baffling to the haulier; at Bristol, if timber were off-loaded from ship to quay, a loading charge was made, but if it were loaded straight on to a vehicle there was no charge, so Wickham and Norris bought 16 two-wheeled trailers and a couple of Fordson tractors; the timber was off-loaded from ship to trailer and moved at the merchants' convenience.

division. For the application of division (3) the country was divided into three grades: (a) important industrial centres and principal ports; (b) other industrial centres and (c) rural areas.

In the London area, apart from attendants and mates there were five categories of driver and the wages laid down varied from 54s a week for vehicles under 1ton carrying capacity to 72s or 73s for vehicles over five tons capacity. Mates were to be paid 57s or 59s on steam wagons.

Trunk drivers were to be paid 60s on vehicles under 2ton capacity, 65s up to 12ton gross weight and 70s over 12ton and up to 22ton gross. Mates' pay was 56s.

In the third class wages varied from 45s for a man driving a vehicle of under 30cwt capacity in a grade 3 area to 70s for the driver of a vehicle over 12ton gross in a grade 1 area. For purely agricultural services 10% less than grade 3, with a minimum of 45s could be paid. Mates' wages varied from 48s to 56s. Wages for youths and attendants under 21 depended on the length of service as well as grade and varied from 30s to 47s 6d.

It soon became evident that these scales were unenforceable, except where the unions had the majority of a firm's drivers in membership and such firms were a tiny minority of the total number of employers. There was no power of inspection of employers' records by the Board. If it is asked why did not the licensing authorities search out defaulters, the answer is that with all the problems they had to

contend with in this formative period, it would have been impossible, especially as even they had no power to order the production of wage books. The result was that those employers who honestly tried to work to the agreement were undercut in their quotations by those who did not. Matters were not helped by long-drawn arguments about grading which were not finally settled in some areas until October 1936.

In this impasse, the Minister of Labour (Ernest Brown) appointed an independent committee to examine the situation. The chairman was Sir James B. Baillie and the other members Sir Gerald Bellhouse and John Forster. The committee's report, laid before Parliament in May 1937, recommended that members of both the central and the area boards should be nominated by the Minister, after consultation with the appropriate bodies and that to the central boards should be added three independent members having no connection whatever with the industry, one of these to be chairman. The committee recommended that Scotland should no longer have a separate central board. The reconstituted board should have statutory powers to fix minimum wages for 'A' and 'B' licence holders.

Despite strong objections from the organisations representing ancillary users, the committee urged that the wages of the drivers employed by C licence holders should also be controlled, but by different machinery. Several possible methods of doing this were set out in the report.

The government accepted the committee's recommendations and incorporated them in a Bill, which, after a few amendments, became the Road Haulage Wages Act 1938. It got over the problem of 'C' licensees by giving legal force to any agreement about wages and conditions of drivers employed by ancillary users, where those making the agreement represented a substantial body of both employers and workers in the trade. Wages and conditions not less favourable to the workers than those authorised by the Central Board would also be acceptable. A right of appeal to the Industrial Court in cases of doubt was given. Road transport employees of the railway companies were excluded from the Act, because of the special negotiating machinery already in existence for them.

All representative members of the Central and Area Boards were to be nominated by the Minister after consultation with representative bodies of employers and workers. The Central Board was to consist of: (a) not less than 12 nor more than 18 representative members, equally divided between employers and workers; (b) two members from each area board in England and from Scotland, also equally divided and (c) not less than three nor more than five independent members, one of whom was to be appointed by the Minister as chairman and one as deputy chairman.

Above left: *The author in 1938.*

Above: *G. W. Quick Smith ('QS'), when assistant secretary of the London & Home Counties Haulage Contractors Association (which he had joined in 1935), became also secretary of the National Conference of Express Carriers, then of the Standing Joint Committee of Hauliers' National Organisations; when the associations were reorganised in 1944, he was appointed secretary of the National Road Transport Federation; following the passing of the Transport Act 1947, he became Chief Secretary and Legal Adviser to the Road Haulage Executive of the British Transport Commission and later, Chief Executive of the Transport Holding Company and then Deputy Chairman and Chief Executive of the National Freight Corporation.*

Right: *There was intense rivalry between the TGWU and the United Road Transport Workers when the unions were fighting against wage reductions; the cost of living figures are related to 1914.*

The Act came into force on 1 January 1939 and it soon became apparent that the independent members would be the dominant factor. To put it bluntly, for the next 30 years, wages in the haulage industry were fixed by people who had no practical knowledge of its operations and did not have to find the money to foot the bill. Bevin, who, as much as anyone, was

THE UNITED ROAD TRANSPORT WORKERS' ASSOCIATION OF ENGLAND

LATE UNITED CARTERS AND MOTORMEN'S ASSOCIATION OF ENGLAND
AFFILIATED TO THE TRADES UNION CONGRESS

Central Office :

126 Upper Brook Street,

C.-on-M., MANCHESTER.

A. HILTON, General Secretary.

Telephone No. 6334 City.

Reg. No. 711 T.U.   Approved Society under the National Health Insurance Act—No. 1732.

Comparative Statement Shewing the Differences Between :

(a) **Transport and General Workers' Agreement, dated 6th December, 1922.**

(b) **UNITED ROAD TRANSPORT WORKERS' AGREEMENT, dated 10th August, 1921.**

(c) **New Proposals of Employers, dated July, 1923.**

1. Rates of Wages when Cost of Living is 65 per cent.

	Under T. & G.W. Agreement.		Under U. R. T. W. Agreement.		Under New Proposals.
One Horse Drivers	50/-	......	53/-	......	51/-
Two Horse Drivers	54/-	......	58/-	......	55/-
Stable and Garage Hands	50/-	......	53/-	......	51/-
Steam Wagon Drivers	62/-	......	66/-	......	63/-
Steam Wagon Steerers	52/-	......	55/-	......	53/-
Petrol W. Drivers, 2 tons and over	59/-	......	63/-	......	60/-
Petrol W. Drivers, under 2 tons	54/-	......	56/-	......	55/-
Ford, up to 1 ton, Adults	50/-	......	No Rate	......	51/-
Ford, up to 1 ton, Youths	40/-	......	No Rate	......	41/-
Petrol Assistants and Loaders	50/-	......	53/-	......	51/-

2. Rate of Payment for Week-end (Sunday) Ostling.

	Each Visit.		Each Visit.		Each Visit.
One to Four Horses	1/-	......	1/6	......	1/-
Five Horses	1/3	......	1/6	......	1/3
Six Horses	1/6	......	1/6	......	1/6
Seven Horses	1/9	......	1/9	......	1/9
Eight Horses	2/-	......	2/-	......	2/-

3. BASIC RATE to which Wages may be reduced (i.e., when Cost of Living is ZERO).

One Horse Driver	37/-	......	40/-	......	38/-
Two Horse Drivers	41/-	......	45/-	......	42/-
Stable and Garage Hands	37/-	......	40/-	......	38/-
Steam Wagon Drivers	49/-	......	53/-	......	50/-
Steam Wagon Steerers	39/-	......	42/-	......	40/-
Petrol W. Drivers, 2 tons and over	46/-	......	50/-	......	47/-
Petrol W. Drivers, under 2 tons	41/-	......	43/-	......	42/-
Ford, up to 1 ton, Adults	37/-	......	No Rate	......	38/-
Ford, up to 1 ton, Youths	27/-	......	No Rate	......	28/-
Petrol Assistants and Loaders	37/-	......	40/-	......	38/-

Express Co-operative Printing Co., Ltd., (T.U. 46 Hrs.), 17 *Blackfriars Street, Manchester.*   23123

responsible for the Act, regarded it as only a temporary measure until both sides of the industry were sufficiently well organised to make binding agreements without external intervention, but the Central Board hung on long after its decisions had become of little more than academic interest, because inflation in the late 1960s and the shortage of good drivers forced most employers to pay well above the Board's minima.

Nothing was said in the awards of either the Conciliation Board or the Road Haulage Wages Board about sickness and my Red Arrow drivers must have been alone in the industry in receiving full pay during illness for an unlimited period. Unfortunately as the staff grew, I found that this privilege was being abused. The strict interpretation and enforcement of the Wages Act deprived us of the former 'give and take' between employer and employee and, as sickness payments had by 1939 become a burden (since none of my competitors paid in this way), the privilege was not extended to new employees from then on.

Another unusual feature of Red Arrow operation from 1935 was the institution of a five-day week for collection and delivery drivers without loss of pay. The vans engaged in this work were divided into groups of five and to each group a leading driver without a van of his own but who knew all the five rounds was appointed. No one worked on Sundays and each man had one weekday off in turn — Monday one week, Tuesday the next and so on, with the leading driver doing his round on that day. It was part of the agreement that each man, on his day off, should telephone the office at 9 am. Should some other driver not have shown up for duty, he would then, if required, go into work and, of course, be paid at overtime rates for the day. This unusual arrangement ensured that our terminal services were never disrupted.

Below: *At an Associated Road Operators' dinner at Shrewsbury in 1938; (left to right, standing), Joe Male, Scott Hall, J. W. Beresford, Roger Sewill, G. F. Goodwin, L. Patrick; (seated), A. Lessbrooks, Mrs Palmer, Mrs Loosemore, C. A. Loosemore; Male was one of the first Black Country operators in 1919; Scott Hall (as 'S. T. R.') wrote articles on costs for* The Commercial Motor *for many years; Beresford, the area chairman, was head of Beresford, Caddy & Pemberton of Tunstall; Roger Sewill, then director of ARO, was earlier the founder of London & Southern Counties Transport; Goodwin was area secretary and Patrick his assistant; Loosemore was sub-area chairman.*

Chapter 9

It is not unfair to say that the thousands of men who tried to make a living out of haulage in 1919 and the following years had no idea what they ought to charge for their services, except to offer a lower rate than the potential customer was already paying. Indiscriminate competition of this sort not only led to numerous bankruptcies among hauliers, but, in the end, destroyed the railway rates system and made it impossible for the railways to perform their obligations to traders.

Although the Surrey Iron Railway (1801) — the first public railway ever sanctioned — had a simple classification of goods (as did some of the canals which preceded it), it was not until 1888 that a standard classification, with maximum rates, was made legally binding on all British railways. The principle was recognised of charging 'what the traffic will bear' and eight classes were instituted, based on: (a) the value of the commodity; (b) the cost of handling; (c) damageability; (d) the method of packing; (e) size or bulk in relation to weight.

It is important to note that while the cost of handling was a factor to be taken into account when deciding classification, the cost of conveyance was not.

The Railway & Canal Traffic Act, 1894, made the rates in force on 31 December 1892 the maxima unless the railways could prove the reasonableness of an increase. The final decision lay with the Railway & Canal Commission, established in 1873. So far from obtaining substantial increases beyond the 1892 figures, the railways were forced, for a variety of reasons, to grant thousands of 'exceptional' rates, ie rates below the authorised maxima. An Act of 1854 forbade the railways to give 'undue preference' to any trader and this meant, in effect, that if one customer in a district were given an exceptional rate for his traffic, then all persons in that district engaged in the same trade were entitled to ask for the same rate.

In the 20 years to 1914, so many exceptionals were created that the statutory schedules and classification were obsolete. The framers of the 1921 Act, which formed the four amalgamated railway companies, attempted to remedy this by expanding the number of classes so as to bring all traffic (except coal, coke and patent fuel) under one or other of 21 classes. Those responsible for the classification were told to have

regard to the following factors, which, it will be seen, vary slightly in detail and order from those of 1888-92: (a) the value of the commodity; (b) its bulk in comparison with its weight; (c) the risk of damage; (d) the cost of handling; (e) the saving of cost when merchandise is carried in large quantities.

This classification only applied to goods traffic. Articles sent by passenger train were carried either at company's risk or owner's and there were different scales for perishable and non-perishable articles. Non-perishables were dived into 13 groups.

The actual charges for both goods and passenger traffic were based on tapering mileage. The taper was very pronounced in passenger train traffic, where the maximum charge was reached at 300 miles.

'What the traffic will bear' meant that the goods with the highest intrinsic value were put in the highest class. In most cases such goods are not unduly bulky and it was very easy for hauliers to make serious inroads into all the higher classified traffic. This might have been justified even on the basis of the hauliers' costs if these had been known, but most were guessing all the time. Because of the doctrine of 'undue preference' there was a ready sale for a volume compiled annually by a Midland publishing firm. This set out all the exceptional rates authorised from every goods receiving station in the country and was a useful guide to hauliers carrying general cargo.

As a means to combat road competition, the Road & Rail Traffic Act, 1933, authorised the railways to make agreements with any customer to carry all his traffic at a flat rate. There is something to be said for flat rates if they are calculated following a careful study of the customer's dispatches over a lengthy period and are no more than an averaging out of the total charges on the normal basis. They can save an enormous amount of work in invoicing, but are dangerous unless fluctuations in the average weight of consignments are watched. The railways in the 1930s used flat rates very effectively in defence of their traffic. A variation on the flat rate idea was tried in Scotland. On the three most heavily trafficked routes (Glasgow-Dundee; Glasgow-Perth and Glasgow-Aberdeen) all traffic in classes 7 to 20, if offered in minimum lots of four tons, was carried at special rates which, although including collection and delivery, were

During the late 1920s and the 1930s, Leyland named its chassis after animals; here are the Octopus (with eight wheels, of course), above left; the Badger (to carry 5ton) left; and the smaller Cub above; one version of which was also used for buses; Taylor's Octopus, oddly enough for so large a vehicle in 1938, had a petrol engine.

so low that they were below the standard Class 7 station to station rates. So many exceptionals were granted that by the mid-1930s the classification of 1921 had become meaningless.

The 1933 Act, following the Salter Report, also included a provision for the establishment of a Transport Advisory Council. This was a body nominated by the Minister of Transport to represent the following interests:

Local authorities in England and Wales (4); local authorities in Scotland (2); users of mechanically propelled vehicles (5); users of horses and horse-drawn vehicles (1); pedestrians (1); pedal-cyclists (1); railways (3); canals (other than those owned or controlled by the railways) (1); coast-wise shipping (2); harbours and docks (other than those owned or controlled by the railways) (1); labour (3); trading interests, including agriculture (5). When the Council was formed Sir Arthur Griffith-Boscawen was appointed chairman.

In July, 1935, the Council appointed a programme committee to consider investigating some of the points raised by the Salter Conference. This committee suggested an investigation into service and rates in relation to goods traffic by rail, canal, road and coast-wise shipping, starting with road transport. Sixteen members of the Council were appointed as a committee of investigation; they included J. B. Horne (Pickfords) and J. S. Nicholl (McNamara). On the recommendation of the British Road Federation, J. H. Turner (London Cartage Association) was added to the committee. From these a sub-committee was formed consisting of the road and rail representatives.

The sub-committee said that 'the stabilisation of wages, working conditions and rates within the Road Industry requires to be dealt with before serious progress can be made in its relation to other forms of transport'. The wages problem had been dealt with by the Baillie Committee and its report led to the Road Haulage Wages Act, 1938.

On rates, the sub-committee said a structure should be evolved by 'A' and 'B' licence holders taking into account only those factors which affect road transport. They suggested that, in each traffic area, a Rates Committee with statutory powers should be established and a Rates Officer appointed who would have power to approve or modify any rates schedules agreed by the Rates Committee and, in the event of disagreement among members of the Committee, to fix rates. There would be a right of appeal to a Road

Rates Tribunal, consisting of a representative of the hauliers and a representative of the traders with an independent chairman. The tribunal would also deal with matters affecting more than one area where the area rates committees had been unable to agree. Rates approved by the Area Rates Officer would be legally enforceable and would, therefore, be published. Their observance would be a condition attached to a haulier's licence. A similar system of rates control was suggested for canal carriers.

In the light of later developments, it is interesting to note that the railway companies in a memorandum to the Advisory Council on 7 September 1936 said:

'So far as the railway companies can ascertain, the majority of trading interests in the country do not desire fundamental alterations in the railway rates structure and regard the general effect of its practical application as productive of trading stability.

'In the circumstances the railway companies do not ask to be exempted from these obligations, which they consider not inappropriate to a public service, but they

Left: *The interesting point about this vehicle, which appears to be an Associated Daimler and was on the road in 1925, is the shape of the driver's cab, which suggests that it ought to be followed by a coach body; so it was at weekends when the container was lifted off and a coach body was fitted.*

Below: *Two ways of collecting sugar-beet; the Morris-Commercial 'Roadless' of 1925 did not win acceptance.*

think it reasonable to ask that their competitors on the roads should now also accept the position of a public service with the regulations appropriate to the type of service which they now offer'.

The British Road Federation, speaking on behalf of Associated Road Operators, the Commercial Motor Users' Association, the National Association of Furniture Warehousemen & Removers, the National Road Transport Employers' Federation and the Scottish Commercial Motor Users' Federation, in March 1937 put in a very long memorandum, in

which, rather reluctantly it seemed, it came to the conclusion that statutory control of road rates was necessary if stability were ever to be achieved in the transport industry as a whole. If this could be done, a natural division of function on economic grounds would follow, with each form of transport handling the traffic for which it was most fitted. It was the BRF's suggestions for National & Area Rates Advisory Committees working with a Road Rates Tribunal & area Rates Commissioners that prompted the recommendations of the Advisory Council's sub-committee referred to above. As to the basis on which road rates should be calculated, the BRF agreed that cost must be the main factor but, in view of the wide divergencies in costs between hauliers, it suggested that, in the first place, the rates charged by reputable carriers should be taken as the basis for the proposed structure.

Neither the BRF nor the Advisory Council in their reports made any reference to the almost complete absence of any conditions of carriage among road hauliers. A few tonnage carriers referred somewhat vaguely on their notepaper or consignment notes to a limitation of liability, but only the firms long-established in the carriage of parcels and smalls had precise conditions to which the attention of customers was directed. Paradoxically, although this section of the industry is the one where cost is hardest to assess, it was the one which offered the best chance of co-ordination. The necessity usually for handling parcels two or three times between collection and delivery and the near-impossibility of predicting the variation of loadings day by day prevent a parcels carrier from determining the precise cost of carrying an individual parcel, but the very complications of the business limit the number of firms engaged in it, so that the urge to wild rate-cutting which has so often been prevalent among other hauliers has generally been absent from parcel carrying. From the earliest days most parcel carriers published scales of rate charges and, although these were sometimes replaced by specially favourable terms for large customers, the majority were charged scale rates.

It was far different with the general hauliers. Those who rushed into the industry as owner-drivers in the 1920s were concerned first and foremost with raising the money to buy fuel and pay off their hire-purchase loan and many gave little thought to other expenses. Traffic was obtained through doing a job cheaper than it was already being done. Even when a haulier got a good rate for an outward load he often cut someone else's rate to obtain a back load.

Although the trade papers pushed the virtues of road transport at every opportunity, their editors were not blind to the long term effects of such foolishness and consistently urged a proper study of all costs. In

94

this connection tribute must be paid to the work of H. Scott Hall, who, for 36 years (as 'STR') wrote about costs in *The Commercial Motor.* Wherever he could find firms willing to co-operate, he tabulated all their outgoings under a number of headings and related these to mileage, so that he was able to establish tables of recommended charges based on cost for various sizes and types of vehicle. Hall's figures were often criticised as being far too high in practice, but they did serve as a yardstick and his writings must have caused many a haulier to think twice before quoting what might have been an unprofitable rate.

The enormous difference between costs in the period covered by this book and the present day is emphasised by a comparison of the costs of fuel and wages. In 1937, the average price per gallon to commercial users (including tax) was 1s 4d for petrol

Left: *When the Hanson & Holdsworth group established a Birmingham base in 1935, it started a local service besides its Yorkshire trunk and issued this rate card for the collection and delivery of parcels in Birmingham and the Black Country.*

Right: *A reproduction of a page of the Red Arrow 1937 rate book for traffic from Birmingham (see p97).*

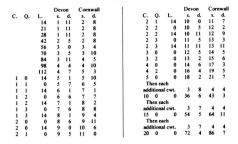

Zones G and H.
Devon and Cornwall.

C.	Q.	L.	Devon s. d.	Cornwall s. d.	C.	Q.	L.	Devon s. d.	Cornwall s. d.
		14	1 11	2 8	2	1	14	10 0	11 7
		21	1 11	2 8	2	2	0	10 5	12 2
		28	1 11	2 8	2	2	14	10 11	12 9
		42	2 5	2 8	2	3	0	11 5	13 3
		56	3 0	3 4	2	3	14	11 11	13 11
		70	3 5	3 10	3	0	0	12 5	14 5
		84	3 11	4 5	3	2	0	13 2	15 6
		98	4 4	4 10	4	0	0	14 6	17 3
		112	4 7	5 3	4	2	0	16 4	19 5
1	0	14	5 1	5 10	5	0	0	18 2	21 7
1	1	0	5 7	6 5			Then each		
1	1	14	6 1	7 1			additional cwt.	3 8	4 4
1	2	0	6 6	7 7	10	0	0	36 6	43 3
1	2	14	7 1	8 2			Then each		
1	3	0	7 6	8 8			additional cwt.	3 7	4 4
1	3	14	8 1	9 4	15	0	0	54 5	64 11
2	0	0	8 6	9 11			Then each		
2	0	14	9 0	10 6			additional cwt.	3 7	4 4
2	1	0	9 5	11 0	20	0	0	72 4	86 7

Zone I.
Hants, Wilts, Dorset and Sussex.

C.	Q.	L.	s. d.	C.	Q.	L.	s. d.	C.	Q.	L.	s. d.
		7	1 2	1	2	0	6 1	3	2	0	12 8
		14	1 6	1	2	14	6 7	4	0	0	13 11
		21	1 10	1	3	0	7 0	4	2	0	15 7
		28	1 11	1	3	14	7 6	5	0	0	17 3
		42	2 5	2	0	0	7 10			Then 3/3 each	
		56	2 11	2	0	14	8 4			additional cwt.	
		70	3 4	2	1	0	8 9	10	0	0	33 6
		84	3 8	2	1	14	9 3			Then 2/10 each	
		98	4 0	2	2	0	9 8			additional cwt.	
		112	4 4	2	2	14	10 1	15	0	0	47 8
1	0	14	4 10	2	3	0	10 6			Then 2/9 each	
1	1	0	5 3	2	3	14	11 0			additional cwt.	
1	1	14	5 8	3	0	0	11 5	20	0	0	61 5

For places in the Isle of Wight add 33⅓%.

Zone J.
(Kent)

Zone L.
(Herts, Beds and Bucks.)

C.	Q.	L.	Kent. s. d.	Herts., Beds. and Bucks. s. d.	C.	Q.	L.	Kent. s. d.	Herts., Beds. and Bucks. s. d.
		14	1 8	1 0	2	1	14	8 7	6 4
		21	1 8	1 2	2	2	0	9 0	6 7
		28	1 8	1 4	2	2	14	9 5	6 11
		42	2 1	1 8	2	3	0	9 10	7 2
		56	2 6	1 11	2	3	14	10 3	7 6
		70	2 11	2 3	3	0	0	10 8	7 9
		84	3 4	2 6	3	2	0	11 5	9 0
		98	3 9	2 9	4	0	0	13 1	10 3
		112	4 1	3 1	4	2	0	14 9	12 0
1	0	14	4 6	3 5	5	0	0	16 5	13 6
1	1	0	4 11	3 8			Then each		
1	1	14	5 4	4 0			additional cwt.	3 4	2 4
1	2	0	5 9	4 3	10	0	0	33 1	25 2
1	2	14	6 2	4 7			Then each		
1	3	0	6 7	4 10			additional cwt.	3 4	2 2
1	3	14	7 0	5 2	15	0	0	49 4	36 0
2	0	0	7 5	5 5			Then each		
2	0	14	7 10	5 9			additional cwt.	3 3	2 1
2	1	0	8 3	6 1	20	0	0	65 7	46 5

Barnet is not reckoned in Zone "L" but is charged as a London suburb (see Zone "K")

and 1s for fuel oil. Wages varied with the size of vehicle. One or two examples will suffice. The National Joint Conciliation Board for the Road Motor Transport Industry (Goods), which was a voluntary organisation without statutory powers, recommended that as from 1 January 1935, the wages of drivers of vehicles of over 2ton and up to 3½ton capacity, based in the principal industrial centres and not on long-distance work, should be 62s 6d for 48 hours. The first Order under the Road Haulage Wages Act, 1938, increased the rate for these men to 65s 6d as from 5 May 1940. London-based drivers of vehicles of over 5ton capacity, under the Conciliation Board's scale, were to receive 72s or 73s according to length of service and 77s or 78s under the Wages Board decision. The Conciliation Board's recommendations were, in practice, only observed by the larger employers and thousands of drivers were paid less during the period we are dealing with.

The Commercial Motor in its issue of 10 May 1946 gave the following cost figures for August 1939:

Payload (in tons)	Standing Charges (per week)	Running Costs (per mile)
2	£4 11s 6d	3.27d
3	£4 17s 9d	3.64d
5	£5 5s 0d	4.37d
6	£5 17s 6d	5.49d
7-8	£6 10s 0d	6.38d

Many attempts were made to get agreement on rates for specific traffics and in specific areas but it is doubtful if any were wholly successful. In February, 1927, after several years of discussion following an abortive attempt in 1921, the principal hauliers in south-west Lancashire agreed to divide traffic to and from the principal Lancashire towns into four classes. Class A was to be for such items as raw cotton in press-packed bales, paper in rolls, crates or bundles and goods for export in press-packed bales or cases. Class B was for commodities such as pneumatic tyres, prepared battens and boards and barbed wire in bundles or rolls. Class C was for loose earthenware, eggs (crated or cased) and wines and spirits in casks or pipes. Class D was for exceptionally bulky items. The lowest charges were to be for Class A. There is no record of how long this agreement lasted.

Perhaps the section of the industry which came nearest to success before the development of inter-working between parcels carriers in the mid-1930s was furniture removing. The West Riding of Yorkshire had an effective agreement for local movements, which were taken to be those where the out and home journey could be made in a day. In 1937 the Employers' Panel of the Yorkshire Traffic Area Joint Conciliation Board, following the recommendations of the Transport Advisory Council, got to work on the preparation of a rates structure for general haulage and asked the local centres of the Removers' Association to produce rates for removals up to 400 miles.

L. W. Morton of Grimshaw & Evans (already mentioned in Chapter 6 in connection with Transport Service) put forward a formula based on collection charges of 8s an hour for a van and two men, with 2s an hour for each additional man, or, alternatively, a flat rate of £2 10s and the same charges for delivery with trunking charges based on mileage. These would be 6d a mile for a van of 30cwt unladen weight and 600cu ft capacity; 8d for 2ton and 750cu ft and 1s for three tons and 1,000cu ft. These figures were not universally accepted and, in the end, all such discussions were terminated by the march of events, but the details are interesting as indicating costs at that time.

The idea of fixing road rates with statutory authority was not new. An Act of 1691, which was only repealed in 1867, required the magistrates of each county at the first sessions after Easter each year 'to assess and rate the prices of all land carriage of goods' moving within their jurisdictions and to have tables of rates prominently displayed in some public place.

The problem in modern times was not so much concerned with local work as with long distance movements and hauliers who discussed possible solutions in the 1930s were interested to read of a similar situation in the United States, where it was complicated by the much greater distances covered by road transport even then. James Paterson, of Carter, Paterson went to America in 1938 and on his return circulated a report on this matter.

The Federal Motor Carriers Act, 1935, empowered the Interstate Commerce Commission (which already controlled railroad rates) to control interstate road rates by approving or disallowing schedules compulsorily deposited with it by all hauliers operating across state boundaries. Once approved, schedules were binding on both operator and traders and the Commission's Bureau of Motor Carriers had an enforcement staff to see that they were. The Commission did not itself lay down any classification but the American Trucking Association prepared a comprehensive classification which was widely adopted by hauliers. In some states there was also control of internal rates and in these cases, the states laid down a classification. Massachusetts had one

Below: The smallest vehicle AEC has ever produced was the 2-tonner first offered in 1924; the LNER was using this one in 1926 for local collection and delivery work; it still only had oil-lighting and as the law then stood, was limited to 16mph; the unladen weight of 3ton 3cwt 2qr was high for a payload of only 2ton.

Below right: With the aid of a magnifying glass, it is possible to read that this solid-tyred Thornycroft type KC was repainted in 1937, although it was already obsolete at that date; being on solid tyres and weighing 4ton 9cwt 2qr its speed limit was 16mph; the inscription on the side of the cab suggests that the owners were prepared to hire the vehicle out.

based on volume and also taking cost into account.

Paterson observed that, although the activities of the Commission had led to standard conditions for inter-state traffic and had encouraged the stabilisation of road rates at a common level, there had been little effort to relate rates to operating costs. They appeared, generally, to approximate to a little below rail rates. A great difficulty was that taxes and wages varied from state to state.

As already mentioned road transport in Northern Ireland, except for purely local movements and own-account operators, was nationalised under an Act of 1935 and the Northern Ireland Road Transport Board, which was formed to manage the new undertaking, had as one of its first tasks to devise a classification for merchandise. There were five classes. Classes A, B and C, the lowest rated classes, were all for basic materials and were subject to a minimum of 2tons for Class A and of one ton for Classes B and C. Most manufactured goods came into Classes D and E where there was no minimum but a smalls scale for consignments not exceeding 3cwt. Rates were based on mileage and, for goods in Classes A, B and C did not include loading and/or unloading. All scheduled rates were for conveyance at owner's risk; a surcharge of 25% was made if the Board were required to accept liability. There were special scales for furniture (not including household removals), agricultural implements and machines, luggage, cycles and perambulators, dead pigs, fish from the ports, buttermilk in runlets and live animals. Classification appears to have been on the basis of 'what the traffic will bear'. The board's conditions of carriage included special conditions relating to goods passing from Northern Ireland to the Free State. There were also special conditions for the conveyance of livestock.

When interworking between express carriers began to develop on a national scale in the 1930s, it was several years before a method of charging was developed which was fair to all parties concerned. The failure of L. W. Morton's Transport Service has been explained in a previous chapter as being largely due to the use of a mileage scale for charging, irrespective of locality and the charges made by the other carriers involved. I made the same mistake in launching Red Arrow Deliveries in December, 1933, but after 18 months a fundamental change was made. As near as is possible with parcel work (and, of course, without computer assistance) an estimate was made of costs broken down into (a) collection and sorting, (b) trunking, (c) delivery after sorting. The country was then divided into zones, each zone being an area covered from a Red Arrow depot or from the depot of an associated carrier. For collection and delivery costs, scales were worked out according to weight. Trunking was calculated on aggregate tonnage. Thus from 10 June 1935, each rate to a customer was made up of three parts so that where Red Arrow performed

Above left: *Early morning at the Birmingham Wholesale Market in 1932; Baragwanath's lorry was a Commer Centaur; both names are interesting; Commercial Cars Ltd was in business at the beginning of the century and noteworthy then for the use of an epicyclic gearbox with preselector; Centaur was a Coventry firm in the Humber group, which obtained control of Commer in 1926.*

Left: *United Automobile Services, with headquarters at Darlington, operates bus services over much of north-eastern England; prior to nationalisation it also had a parcel service which was not confined to the buses but employed a fleet of vans and operated a trunk service to Leeds; this 50cwt Bedford was one of its collection and delivery vans in 1936.*

Above: *Cowan & Company were, for many years, cartage agents for the railways in north-eastern England; the interesting point about this 1938 6ton Foden is that they got the weight down to 2ton 9cwt, so that it could operate at 30mph.*

both collection and trunking, but another carrier delivered, the throughout rate consisted of charges for the Red Arrow services, plus a delivery charge based on an agreed scale. The same principle also applied where Red Arrow only collected and another carrier both trunked and delivered or where another trunked and and a third delivered. The same agreement applied, of course, in the reverse direction. The bulk tonnage rate for trunking recalls the long-standing arrangement which Atlas Express and others had with the railways.

Classification among smalls carriers was rudimentary. It usually consisted, as in the case of Red Arrow, of having standard rates and putting a surcharge on for goods which were either very bulky or very fragile. The Red Arrow surcharge was usually 20%. Some concerns, such as Carter, Paterson and Pickfords, also had a slightly lower scale than standard for customers with a substantial flow of regular traffics. Some examples of rates schedules are in the appendices.

Following the views of the Transport Advisory Council it became government policy in the late 1930s to introduce statutory rates for road transport and, with this in view, first the Express Carriers and then the road side of the Road and Rail Central Conference spent many hours trying to devise an equitable scheme. The most promising idea was that put forward by N. D. Fawkner, general manager of Carter, Paterson. He suggested that all traffic carried by road might be divided into six classes, the allocation of any particular traffic being determined by the relative importance of the following factors: (a) bulkiness; (b) stowage; (c) 'what the traffic will bear'; (d) risk to the goods themselves; (e) carrier's liability for damage to other goods, plant and men; (f) awkwardness of handling; (g) use of special plant; (h) seasonal nature of the traffic or any other special considerations.

Had this or some similar formula been adopted it would then have been necessary to relate it to the actual costs of operation and the result might have been very different from any revised system of railway charging, unless the revolutionary step had been taken of adapting rail rates to road costs.

Chapter 10

Solid tyres for all ordinary purposes had almost disappeared by 1939, even on steamers. There were still 'locomotives' on the roads with steel tyres but they had become confined to such work as forestry, where their movements did not involve great mileage and rough ground had to be traversed.

It was in the 1930s that the steamer reached its peak of efficiency and driver-comfort. The Sentinels of the decade had a bunker in the cab roof with self-stoking mechanism and a dynamo provided current for electric lighting and the speedometer, for cylinder lubrication and a tyre pump. By 1933 the range included a rigid 8-wheeler to carry 14ton, a 6-wheeler for 12ton and a 4-wheeler for 7ton. Foden and the Yorkshire Patent Steam Waggon Co also produced attractive vehicles in this decade.

For the weightier loads, the latest steam wagon in 1930 could not be beaten for power and fuel economy by any petrol lorry then available and even in the medium range it could hold its own. There were, of course, the drawbacks of finding adequate water supplies, the extra skill required to get the best out of the vehicle and the high ratio of tare weight to load, but the steamer was killed, first by the change in taxation which penalised the heaviest vehicles from 1 January 1934 and then, in the later 1930s, by the development of the high-speed lightweight compression-ignition engine.

Although Britain cannot claim to be the birthplace of this automotive system, its development to reliability and efficiency is perhaps due more to British engineers than to any others, although the first diesel vehicles (as they were soon called) which appeared here were imported. Thus a Mercedes-Benz 5-tonner appeared in May, 1928 and was offered at a chassis price of £1,685, a high figure for those times.

British development came from the successful use of small marine diesels, notably the 40-cylinder 40hp engine produced by Gardner in 1929 and fitted into one of T. H. Barton's buses which ran between Nottingham and Birmingham. Also in 1929, a Kerr-Stuart 7-tonner appeared with a 4-cylinder McLaren-Benz engine. In December of that year Watts of Lydney converted a petrol-engined bus. In the following year, Frank Duston of Leeds converted an S type Leyland using a 50hp Gardner engine and

Sheffield Corporation put a Karrier bus with Benz engine into service. From then on all the leading manufacturers of heavy vehicles began to offer diesel engines as alternatives to petrol and, while most of these were Gardners to start with, some makers developed their own and engines also began to come from specialist firms. The most notable of these was the business started in Peterborough in 1932 by Frank Perkins when he left Aveling and Porter (a famous firm for steam rollers) where he had been managing director.

The 1933 Budget not only hit the steamer, but the diesel vehicle too, by greatly increasing the vehicle duty, although, for the time being, the diesel was left with the tax advantage of only attracting an impost of 1d a gallon on derv against 8d on petrol. The heavier duty on unladen weight was an added incentive in the search for lighter engines and chassis. In January 1935, the tax on derv was increased to that on petrol.

About the middle of the 1930s articulation began to be more seriously considered and by 1939 there was a clear decline in the number of drawbar trailers to be seen on the roads. The development of automatic couplings by Scammell contributed greatly to the growing interest in articulation and legislation gave an impetus in that direction. The 1930 Act made the employment of an 'attendant' obligatory when a trailer was being drawn and this man's wages, like the driver's came under statutory control after the passing of the Road Haulage Wages Act. Mates were originally employed for trailer work in the days when the brakes on the trailer were applied by winding a

Above right: *4 May 1934; a farewell parade of Peek, Frean's last 12 horses beside one of the Scammell mechanical horses that superseded them; production of these highly manoeuvrable 3-wheelers had begun the year before, mainly inspired by the desire of the railways to replace their great stock of horses; there was a 6ton version as well as the 3ton.*

Right: *A useful piece of co-operation when Pickfords hired Norman E. Box's 32-wheel trailer, claimed to be the world's largest, to carry an 84ton stator in April 1937, a late date to see a steam traction engine on the London streets.*

Above: *Karrier, like Scammell, also devised a mechanical horse (in this case called the Cob), which could be adopted for a variety of uses, such as moving tramlines on a semi-trailer with four-in-line rear axle from the Leeds tram depot in Swinegate; the lines are being loaded by a crane drawing its power from the overhead line.*

Below: *Yorkshire wagons had their boilers (double-ended) across the front, in contrast to the other makes of steamer; this is a six-tonner introduced in 1926; it still had the engine in the cab but dry sump lubrication was adopted and Joy valve gear replaced the Hackworth; chain-drive to the rear axle was retained.*

On the truck side:

BRITISH MERCEDES-BENZ LTD.,
37, DAVIES STREET, LONDON. W.1.
THIS 5 TON LORRY RUNNING ON CRUDE OIL ABOUT 4ᴰ PER GALLON.

Above: *Pictures of Mercedes-Benz lorries actually in service are rare, because few were sold in this country, although the British company of that name, starting in 1928, did more perhaps than anyone else to develop interest in the possibilities of compression-ignition; Bosch fuel injection contributed largely to the successful operation of the early diesels; unfortunately, higher taxation in 1933 took away some of their advantages, but even so they scored in better fuel consumption figures.*

Below: *The first Bedfords, 2-tonners classified WHG (short-wheelbase) and WLG (long), appeared in 1931, to be followed the following year by the WS 30cwt model, which was ceremonially launched, as seen here; complete factory-built dropside trucks of the first two models cost only £240 or £260, according to wheelbase; the WS cost as a dropside truck £210.*

Four most interesting pictures showing the emergence of the Karrier Cob; on 21 February 1930 a 1926 Morris-Cowley, fitted with coupling gear designed in the London Midland & Scottish Railway's works at Wolverton, was tested with a horse-dray adapted for use with it; then a Cob embodying a Jowett 2-cylinder horizontally opposed water-cooled engine was tried in the yard at Wolverton and on 24 October 1930 on the road; the final product, to haul $2\frac{1}{2}$ ton, seems to have had some modifications, eg the handbrake position was changed.

wheel in the cab of the motor and so pulling the brakes on by cable. By 1939, more sophisticated control of trailer brakes had been achieved and the 'attendant' had become redundant as a brakesman, although another 20 years passed before the law recognised this. It was the development of articulation that made the carrying of abnormal indivisable loads almost commonplace compared with the excitement when Box's 100-tonner first made its appearance.

An interesting application of articulation was the appearance in 1930 of the Karrier Cob, a small 3-wheeled tractor designed to replace the horse in railway yards and other confined areas and for delivery work in narrow town-centre streets. Its great manoeuvrability made it very successful. In 1933, Scammell also brought out a 3-wheeled mechanical horse, capable of towing up to 6ton loads on semi-trailers and, like the Cob, being able to get into many tight corners.

At the same time, the use of multi-wheelers was growing. It is perhaps, difficult to realise now that a 4 to 5ton lorry could be regarded as adequate for regular

trunking work and that parcels carriers were usually employing 30cwt or 2ton vans for collection and delivery until the late 1930s. Most inter-depot work with 'smalls' was done with 5 or 6ton vans. Not only was the overall volume of traffic less than it is today, but the impact of wages was much less too. As Britain pulled out of the depression, consignments began to increase in size and weight and where articulation did not appeal to an operator, the use of more wheels often did. The 1931 Construction and Use Regulations limited the length of a 4-wheeler to 27ft 6in, of a rigid vehicle with more than four wheels to 30ft and of an articulated vehicle to 33ft. The maximum length for a trailer was 22ft. The unladen weight of a 'heavy motor car' (ie a vehicle exceeding $2\frac{1}{2}$ton unladen) was limited to $7\frac{1}{4}$ton with four wheels, 10ton with six wheels and 11ton with more than six wheels. Total weights laden were limited to 12ton for 4-wheelers, 19ton for 6-wheelers and 22ton for vehicles with more than six wheels or for a tractor-trailer combination. It will be seen that if vehicles were built to the maximum permissible unladen weight, 4-wheelers were limited to $4\frac{3}{4}$tons payload, 6-wheelers to 9tons and larger vehicles to 11. In practice, of course, most four-wheelers weighed considerably less than $7\frac{1}{4}$tons unladen, but, nevertheless, 6-wheelers, with the extra permissible length, often proved more economical to operate where regular loads of 11-12tons were available.

Considerable improvements were made in the 1930s in working conditions for drivers. All-enclosed cabs (although without heating) became general; electric lighting replaced oil or acetylene; screen-wipers more or less efficiently worked electrically were adopted on most vehicles; heavier types had power-assisted steering and hydraulic braking to ease the physical effort.

With vans the big change was from timber to composite or all-metal bodies which greatly reduced tare weights and so increased the maximum carrying capacity permissible within the limits of the statutory overall maxima.

Left: *A rare picture of a Mercedes in the service of a parcel carrier; Gamman & Dicker Ltd served Kent and Sussex and, like many other operators of the time, had a London base under the railway arches in Silwood Street, Bermondsey, not always easy to manoeuvre in and out of; other makes in the Gamman & Dicker fleet were Albion and Leyland.*

Right: *Checking to see if the hops have hit the bridge in Woolwich Road, Charlton; a Carrimore artic based on the Bedford 2ton short chassis was very useful for such light but bulky loads.*

D RACING
STADIUM
SATUR
P. M.
PHONE 2071
PHILLIPS
MOTORS, LTD
IDSTONE
Bedford
BKK 696

Above: *PX, the Rushden parcel carrier used Bedfords modified for articulation not only for household removals but also for inter-depot working.*

Chapter 11

The campaign for a 'Square Deal', which the railways had been planning during 1937, was launched in January 1938, when in a booklet entitled *Clear the lines* and with considerable press publicity, they demanded the abolition of classification and the obligation to publish rates and an end to the doctrine of 'undue preference'. They contended that, only when the railways were free to make such charges as they thought fit, could there be any co-ordination between them and the road carriers. The demand for freedom appeared to hauliers to be a complete volte-face from their position in September, 1936.

The report of the Transport Advisory Council in 1937, with its insistence on road transport producing a rates structure which could be statutorily enforced, was considered at a meeting held in Leeds on 14 December 1937, when representatives of employers in Yorkshire, Lancashire and the West Midlands were present. This meeting, plus the prompting of the British Road Federation, led to a conference in London on 27 January 1938 of representatives of ARO, the CMUA, the NAFW and R and the NRTEF. W. A. Winson, president of the CMUA and chairman of SPD, the Unilever transport subsidiary, was voted to the chair. F. G. Bristow, secretary of the CMUA, agreed to act as honorary secretary. The conference decided to form a Liaison Committee on Rates and the associations were invited to nominate three members each, except the Furniture Removers, who only wanted one.

The status of the Committee was enhanced when, on 9 February 1938, the Minister of Transport announced that he accepted the TAC's recommendations, but when the committee met next day it had a setback, as the ARO representatives did not attend, on the ground that the committee was duplicating the Operators' Committee of the BRF. This was the official reason for the abstention but, in fact, ARO was concerned about the dual character of the CMUA, (which included many ancillary users) and objected to Winson being chairman of the liaison committee. The committee (which had been joined by the Scottish CMUA) had a meeting with officials of the Ministry of Transport on 23 February 1938 for a general exchange of views. At its meeting on 10 March 1938, Winson resigned the chairmanship and was replaced by W. Edwards of the NRTEF. Later

Winson resigned from the committee altogether. In May the National Conference of Parcels Carriers (as it then was) joined the committee. It was allowed four members as were also ARO, the CMUA and the NRTEF. Later, the Scottish Carriers and Haulage Contractors' Association started to send a representative also.

The committee, on 17 June 1938, appointed a sub-committee to consider the standard conditions of carriage which the Parcels Carriers were drawing up and it also decided to call a national conference of two delegates of each association from each traffic area.

This conference was held at the RAC on 19 July 1938, when it was decided to set up area committees and general approval was given to the standard conditions proposed by the liaison committee. To satisfy ARO, it was agreed that the liaison committee's address should be that of the BRF, 120 Pall Mall.

On 29 December 1938, the sub-committee which had been dealing with conditions of carriage held an informal meeting with the railway general managers, who, by then were actively pursuing the 'Square Deal' agitation. At the meeting of the full liaison committee on 6 January 1939, there was some criticism of the sub-committee for exceeding its terms of reference, but eventually authority was given for the negotiations to continue and the sub-committee was strengthened for this purpose, so that it consisted of W. Edwards (Chairman), J. W. Beresford and R. W. Sewill (Associated Road Operators), C. Barrington and C. Holdsworth (Commercial Motor Users' Association), C. S. Dunbar and N. D. Fawkner (National Conference of Express Carriers), R. H. Faro and J. H. Turner (National Road Transport Employers' Federation) and T. Worsley (Scottish Commercial Motor Users' Association). F. G. Bristow (CMUA) acted as secretary of the sub-committee, as well as of the main committee. At most of the sub-committee's meetings, Harold Elliott (Pickfords) and J. S. Nicholl (McNamara) were present by invitation.

Some important concessions were made by the railways as a result of discussions with this sub-committee. They agreed to continue the obligation to obtain the approval of the Railway Rates Tribunal to any alteration in their conditions of carriage until such time as there were common conditions for all forms of transport. They agreed, that, if they obtained their freedom in regard to charges, then for two years after this came into force, they would not object to renewals of existing 'A' and 'B' licences, to the grant of additional 'A'-licensed vehicles to existing hauliers or to the grant to existing hauliers of additional 'B' licences with a limited operating radius of 25 miles.

They proposed the establishment of a Central Consultative Committee of road and rail representatives (with Regional Committees, if thought necessary) to formulate voluntary agreements on rates. The road representatives pointed out that such agreements could not be enforced without statutory machinery and asked that the Bill to repeal the restrictions on railway charges should include clauses for this purpose. The railways would not agree to this, as they considered that the road haulage industry was not yet sufficiently well-organised. They pointed out that it was understood to be the government's intention to introduce a Bill to give effect to the recommendations of the Transport Advisory Council and it would be appropriate if the necessary provisions for enforcement were included with that Bill.

Another conference of national organisations was called for 4.00pm on 6 February 1939 at the RAC preceded by a meeting of the liaison committee at 3.00pm, the purpose being to endorse a memorandum which had been prepared for submission to the TAC jointly by road and rail. The larger meeting did not conclude its business and was adjourned until 10 February, while the liaison committee met again at 7.00pm on the 6th and also on the 9th. The meeting on the 10th eventually endorsed the liaison committee's actions. A copy of the memorandum appears in Appendix 3.

On 4 March 1939, the Railway Companies' Association wrote to the secretary of the liaison

Below: *The Road Traffic Act 1930 permitted a speed of 30mph to vehicles weighing not more than 50cwt; Thornycroft in 1931 produced a Handy chassis which with a 600gal two-compartment aluminium tank and three lengths of hose only weighed 48cwt unladen.*

Right: *What in the days of the horse would be called 'a good pull-up for carmen' became an essential feature of road transport operation in the motor age; 'coffee-shops' (so called even when they were mobile) were soon to be found at strategic spots on all main roads; the ice-cream salesman's tricycle was equally ubiquitous in the London area.*

committee, suggesting that the proposed Central Consultative Committee should consist of 16 members, eight representing the railways and eight the hauliers.

In the curious British way of duplicating activities and then finding a modus vivendi for the resulting division of forces, some leading members of the trade associations, while the liaison committee was negotiating with the railways, decided at a meeting at Frascati's Restaurant on 13 December 1938, to urge the formation of a standing joint committee of hauliers' national organisations to represent 'A' and 'B' licenceholders as distinct from the 'C' members who were then also catered for by some of them. R. P. Bailey of the NRTEF was asked to circulate a resolution to this effect and to invite the associations to meet and support it.

It has not been possible to trace a list of those who were present at this meeting and it seems to have been arranged by the heads of some of the larger firms who had been meeting at the Waldorf Hotel in Aldwych. Rumours about the existence of this group began to circulate round the industry in 1938, but it was very much a secret society and, until after the meeting at Frascati's, direct enquiries of likely participants were met with evasion. Pickfords, McNamara and the Hanson Holdsworth group were certainly involved and Transport Services may have been. I have heard that A. Renwick of Fisher, Renwick attended, but, as I

never met him at any association meeting, I wonder if this could have been so, unless he chose to be an 'eminence grise'.

The associations responded quickly to Bailey's invitation and nominated delegates to a first meeting at the RAC on 26 January 1939, at which it was decided that the Standing Joint Committee should consist of eight representatives from ARO and six each from the CMUA, the NCEC and the NRTEF. The two Scottish associations sent observers but deferred the appointment of delegates.

An executive committee was nominated to consist of J. H. Turner (NRTEF) ex-officio as chairman of the SJC, C. Barrington (CMUA) and J. F. E. Pye (ARO) as vice-chairmen, R. W. Sewill (ARO) as technical adviser plus D. E. Richardson and A. Todd (ARO), F. F. Fowler and L. W. Gupwell (CMUA), C. S. Dunbar and J. Paterson (NCEC) and P. J. R. Tapp and B. G. Turner (BRTEF). G. W. Quick Smith was elected honorary secretary.

Later, the National Association of Furniture Warehousemen and Removers joined the committee with six delegates of whom two (A. Coombs and W. Taylor) were on the Executive. The committee rejected a CMUA proposal that it should include clearing-house representatives. The Scottish CMUA and the Scottish Carriers' & Haulage Contractors' Association eventually joined the committee and nominated J. Strang and I. R. Grove to the executive.

112

Above left: *This is actually a post nationalisation picture but is put in to show a Unipower 4-wheel drive tractor at work; these units were available from 1937.*

Left: *A cartoon which appeared in* Motor Transport *in 1939 after the author had said at a Road-Rail Conference 'That the Lion should lie down with the Lamb has become a fait accompli'.*

Above: *Cliff Warwick built up his business (Broadway Transport) by giving direct delivery from the Vale of Evesham to Smithfield Market, Birmingham; he also went into general haulage and this Commer N5 to carry 5¼ton was in his fleet in 1939; the body was of Duralamin.*

The foundation of the Standing Joint Committee was one of the landmarks in the history of the haulage industry, since it led in the last of the war years to the reorganisation of the employers' organisations, with the present Road Haulage Association as a powerful body representing the professional carriers. Of the personnel, it may be said that the influence of the NRTEF was responsible for the election of J. H. Turner as chairman and G. W. Quick Smith as secretary. Turner was unknown outside London, except, perhaps, among some of the local bodies affiliated to the NRTEF. He was not even a haulier in the ordinary sense, but a contractor for municipal work. He had little appreciation of the difficulties of provincial carriers, but he was able to detect the drift of opinion in a discussion and to sum up the pros and cons so that the issues were clear. More significant was

the appointment of 'QS', as he soon became known, as secretary, so virtually putting him on a par with those leading figures in the industry, Bristow and Sewill. For him, this was a very definite step in a successful career which eventually took him into the top ranks of nationalised transport.

Of the other members of the executive who have not already been mentioned in these pages; Todd had his own business in Yorkshire; Fowler was, like J. H. Turner, a municipal contractor and tipper operator in London; Gupwell had developed a haulage company in Birmingham from a family shopfitting business; Tapp ran a successful meat-carrying concern, Market Transport, and also built van bodies; B. G. Turner was general manager of Thomas Allen, long-established in the Port of London and a subsidiary of Coast Lines.

That the horse had not lost its importance in transport was emphasised at the SJC meeting on 23 February 1939 when a sub-committee was appointed to consider the advisability of licensing horsedrawn vehicles. The move was prompted by two thoughts — the statutory regulation of haulage wages and the necessity, if war broke out, of organising supplies of fodder. At the same meeting a link was arranged with the National Emergency Co-ordination Committee, which was representing the associations in negotiations with the Ministry of Transport on the possibility of war time controls.

Barrington suggested a referendum of members to see if the idea of one association for 'A' and 'B' licensees was welcomed and, although no formal move was made by the meeting, it was obvious that there

Above: *The AEC's Mammoth Major put on the market in 1934, was the first rigid 8-wheeler for civilian use; it was offered with either petrol or diesel engines and with a gross weight of 22ton, could take a pay-load of about 15ton.*

Right: *There are several interesting features about this Albion lorry and trailer; there is an ancient law in the City of London allowing licensed carts to stand for hire at certain points; no carts or their motorised successors ever do stand at these points, but a few firms still register their vehicles each year and are then entitled to display the City's coat of arms; it can be seen in the middle of the firm's name; the inscription in the roundel on the door indicates that the owners are licensed to move bonded goods in the Port of London; the twin-steer 6-wheeler weighing 4ton 19cwt unladen and fitted with a 6-cylinder petrol engine was designed for 10ton loads.*

was a consensus of opinion in favour. This was expressed at a dinner at Kettner's Restaurant on 10 May 1939, when J. H. Watts put forward the idea of a National Federation of three autonomous bodies, one for hauliers, one for ancillary users and one for bus and coach operators. I was present at the dinner and all the emphasis was on the need to organise the professional hauliers in one powerful body. That Watts should have arranged the dinner and put forward the scheme occasioned some surprise. His interests in haulage were small compared with his investments in the Red & White bus group. Red & White was a member of the Tramways, Light Railways and Transport Association, which was unlikely to throw in its lot with a federation largely composed of goods operators. The proposed association for public service operators would, it was obvious, only cater for those independents (mainly small owners) who were already in ARO, the CMUA or the Scottish associations. The suggestion has been made that Watts was acting at the prompting of 'Big Bill' Elliott, the general manager of Pickfords. Pickfords was railway-owned and it would have been to the advantage of the railways to have a single powerful body representing the hauliers in view of the importance attached to joint consultation. Alternatively, Watts might possibly have been inspired

by the Transport Services group, in view of Barrington's proposal already mentioned. But this is running ahead.

Some members of the SJC were strongly of the opinion that the liaison committee on Rates should be detached from the BRF, (the connection had, by this time, become very slender) and should come under the

114

aegis of the SJC. The liaison committee had now reached the stage where it was about to nominate the road panel to form, with the railways, the Central Consultative Committee and some members of the SJC were clearly resentful at being left out. A lively meeting was held on 7 March 1939 at the RAC, when a deputation from the SJC, consisting of five executive members who were not on the liaison committee, supported by some who were, pressed for the appointments to be made by the newer body.

The liaison committee eventually agreed not to make nominations to the consultative committee until the whole matter had been discussed at a special meeting on 21 March when, in addition to the liaison committee, there would be present two additional members from each national organisation and the chairman of each of the area rates committees of the liaison committee.

The outcome of this meeting was that it was agreed that the liaison committee should become a sub-committee of the SJC, that the liaison committee should nominate the road members of the Central Consultative Committee, that the nominations should be ratified by the SJC and that nominations should be solely by ability, irrespective of membership of particular associations.

At its next meeting on 28 March, the liaison committee decided to ask that the road panel of the Consultative Committee (which was to be renamed the Road & Rail Central Conference) should number 12 and, after a ballot, nominated L. B. Andrews, C. Barrington, J. W. Beresford, C. S. Dunbar, H. W. Elliott, G. D. M. Fairclough, N. D. Fawkner, I. R. Grove, C. Holdsworth, J. S. Nicholl, R. W. Sewill and W. Taylor. F. G. Bristow agreed to act as secretary to the panel. Several of these men have already been mentioned; of the others, Andrews had a business in Swansea; Beresford was head of Beresford, Caddy and Pemberton, the 70-year old business in the Potteries already mentioned in connection with Hauliers Ltd in chapter 7; Fairclough was one of a family largely concerned with fruit and vegetable transport in London, whose business had expanded into the Eastern Counties notably through the acquisition of E. R. Ives of Norwich; Grove was head of Film Transport Services and Taylor was wellknown in the removal world as director of Taylor's Depository.

To complete the tie-up, those members of the liaison committee who were not on the Executive of the SJC were on 29 March invited to attend its meetings. These were Fairclough, Fawkner and Nicholl, plus C. H. Clague of Stott's Motors, Oldham, R. H. Faro of Pickfords, H. J. Sharpley (Sheffield Horse and Motor

Above left: Premier Transport is still in existence and its principal, Harold Russett, was, for many years, chairman of the Express Carriers Group of the Road Haulage Association; it bought this Austin 3-tonner in 1939; note the flap on the off-side of the body at the top which could be opened to allow long pipes or similar objects to protrude.

Left: Fodens, with a long tradition in steam, began making diesel lorries in 1931, using Gardner engines; this is a 4-tonner which was on the road in 1937; there were still operators in the 1930s who did not trust the oil-engine and Foden built some vehicles similar to this but with petrol engines.

Above: Having produced a Vixen, Guy also had to have a Fox and here is one photographed in 1938 outside Lambeth Palace; this may have no significance, but Beck & Pollitzer was not only machinery carrier but often provided floats for the Lord Mayor's Show and similar public events; note the Guy emblem on the radiator cap — a Red Indian's head — 'feathers in our cap'.

Owners' Association) and E. G. Whittaker of A. J. Gupwell Ltd, Birmingham. John Strang from Scotland was for a time on the executive and W. Donaldson Wright of Nottingham was also added. Bristow as secretary of the liaison committee was also invited to attend SJC meetings.

At a meeting of the full SJC on 18 April, it was resolved that the National Emergency Co-ordinating Committee should be wound up and its work entrusted to the SJC. A deputation from the National Conference of Road Transport Clearing Houses was received by the Executive on 20 July, but its request for representation on the SJC was again turned down. At the same meeting a sensible suggestion that someone with a knowledge of road and rail rates should be engaged to assist Bristow was deferred until the next meeting, on 25 July, when it was rejected, although the salary proposed was only £500.

Long before this some leaders of the industry urged the Ministry to prepare functional lists of vehicles so that essential services could be maintained in the event of war. The Ministry did put out a booklet in February 1939, outlining a scheme for dividing traffic areas into districts and sub-districts. Operators were invited to

Above: *Mr F. S. Huxham was a courteous Edwardian gentleman who lived on into the 1940s; from Plymouth and a branch depot in Bristol, he provided 'smalls' services over much of Devon and Cornwall; this Scammell rigid-six, with Gardner 6LW engine, is loaded with 1,007 cases of baked beans, weighing 12ton 18cwt; it covered the 133 miles between Bristol and Plymouth at an average fuel consumption of 12mph.*

Above right: *Thomas Tilling, one of the best known names in the bus world, also had a less-publicised haulage business, mainly concerned with bulk loads and based on Searles Road, off New Kent Road, London.*

Right: *Metropolitan Transport Supply was the transport subsidiary of Kearley & Tonge, the London wholesale grocers, and its fleet had a high proportion of flats to carry lift-bodies with 5ton loads; these were comfortably carried on Thornycroft Sturdys, as shown here.*

form groups within these to facilitate fuel rationing and to divide work equitably in the event of war. The Ministry seemed to lay more emphasis on proximity than on function and as progress in forming groups voluntarily was slow, compulsion was used when war broke out on 3 September 1939. The result was that, in many cases, operators found themselves in groups with no mutual interest at all. Then when the Army wanted vehicles, the Ministry permitted them to take a proportion of each group, again without regard to function. One express carrier in Birmingham had the whole of his fleet of 10 vehicles seized, leaving considerable parts of Worcestershire and Warwickshire without any smalls service at all, until, after some months of agitation, he was able to buy a few replacements.

With the nation at war this story must be brought to an end. The achievements of road transport and the influence of the associations during those difficult years needs further research, but, the SJC proved its worth and 1945 saw the long-discussed reorganisation of the associations accomplished. A National Federation to deal with matters of common interest was an umbrella under which were three self-governing bodies, the Road Haulage Association, the Traders' Road Transport Association and the Passenger Vehicle Operators' Association. Of these only the RHA has remained unchanged in structure and functions. An important feature of its constitution from the first was the establishment, at my suggestion, of functional groups. This provision enabled the National Conference of Express Carriers to end its separate existence, although the Furniture Removers decided to stay out of the amalgamation because of their mixed business.

The Road & Rail Central Conference continued its labours during the war years and accumulated an enormous amount of information on flows of traffic and comparative rates between road and rail, but it was all a waste of time. When the railways were nationalised in 1947, the pretence was maintained for a while of controlling their rates, but before many years had passed they had obtained everything they had originally asked for in the 'Square Deal' campaign. On the other hand, postwar governments not only threw overboard the idea of statutorily enforceable road rates, but made any move towards this end impossible through the monopolies and 'fair trading' legislation and the scrapping of carrier's licences.

Appendix 1

Extract from the Road Traffic Act, 1930

19 — (1) With a view to protecting the public against the risks which arise in cases where the drivers of motor vehicles are suffering from excessive fatigue, it is hereby enacted that it shall not be lawful in the case of

(a) any public service vehicle within the meaning of Part IV of this Act;

(b) any heavy locomotive, light locomotive or motor tractor; or

(c) any motor vehicle constructed to carry goods other than the effects of passengers;

for any person to drive or cause or permit any person employed by him or subject to his orders to drive —

(i) for any continuous period of more than five hours and one half; or

(ii) for any continuous periods amounting in the aggregate to more than 11 hours in any period of 24 hours commencing two hours after midnight; or

(iii) so that the driver has not at least ten consecutive hours for rest in any period of 24 hours calculated from the commencement of any period of driving;

Provided that it shall be a sufficient compliance with the provisions of paragraph (iii) if the driver has at least nine consecutive hours for rest in any such period of 24 hours provided that he has an interval of at least twelve consecutive hours for rest in the next following period of 24 hours.

(2) For the purposes of this section —

(a) any two or more periods of time shall be deemed to be a continuous period unless separated by an interval of not less than half-an-hour in which the driver is able to obtain rest and refreshment;

(b) any time spent by a driver on other work in connection with a vehicle or the load carried thereby, including in the case of a public service vehicle any time spent on a vehicle while on a journey in any other capacity than as a passenger, shall be reckoned as time spent in driving;

(c) in the case of a vehicle which is being used in the course of operations of agriculture or forestry a person shall not be deemed to be driving the vehicle or to be spending time on work in connection with the vehicle or the load carried thereby so long as the vehicle is elsewhere than on a road.

(3) The Minister may, on the application of a joint industrial council, conciliation board, or other similar body, or on a joint application by such organisations, representative of employers and workpeople in the industry, as the Minister of Labour may certify to be proper bodies to make such an application, and after referring the matter to the Industrial Court for advice, by order vary the periods of time prescribed in this section, provided that he is of opinion that such variation is not likely to be detrimental to the public safety.

Any order made under this subsection may be revoked or varied by a subsequent order made in like manner and subject to the like conditions.

(4) If any person acts in contravention of this section, he shall be guilty of an offence;

Provided that a person shall not be liable to be convicted under this section if he proves to the court that the contravention was due to unavoidable delay in the completion of any journey arising out of circumstances which he could not reasonably have foreseen.

(5) This section shall not apply to motor vehicles used for fire brigade or ambulance purposes.

Appendix 2

Red Arrow Deliveries Ltd, 1939

Organisation of nation-wide parcels service from Birmingham, with delivery service for incoming traffic throughout the West Midlands.

Birmingham (Yardley) Depot

Local vans

(1) Collection and delivery service every weekday in the Birmingham and Black Country conurbation, South Staffordshire, North Warwickshire and North Worcestershire (twice daily in most of Birmingham); H. W. Hingley of Wolverhampton and Walsall Corporation Transport acted as collection agents in those towns.

(2) Five days weekly to Shrewsbury and Welshpool, where connection was made with the Central and North Wales services of Aberystwyth Carriers; at Shrewsbury connections were made with Harris who served South Shropshire and Cashion for other places in the county.

Trunk services in both directions

(a) operated by Red Arrow (six nights a week)

(1) London — direct to Malt Street (Old Kent Road) depot.

(2) London (Malt Street) via H. G. Currell's depot at St Alban's; Currell served most of Hertfordshire.

(3) London — (Chiswick depot) via St Albans.

(4) London — (Malt Street) via Chiswick.

(5) London via Coventry depot (Minster Road). (Most London journeys were worked by wagon and drawbar trailer.)

(6) Coventry and Leicester with traffic for Blands, Platts and Whiteman (see below).

(7) Bristol depot (Canning Street) via Cheltenham (Cheltenham Traction Co's depot) and Gloucester depot (Merchant's Road) — see also below.

(b) operated jointly by Red Arrow and Blackburn Parcels Express

(8) Blackburn (Stakes Hall); Blackburn Parcels Express served central and north-east Lancashire and the Fylde

(c) operated by other carriers (six nights a week).

(9) Beresford, Caddy and Pemberton — Tunstall (for delivery in north Staffordshire) and Liverpool, carrying transfer traffic for Globe Parcels Express (south-west Lancashire and the Wirral), F. D. Hulse and H. Shepherd (North Wales).

(10) Beresford, Caddy and Pemberton — Tunstall and Manchester carrying transfer traffic for Manchester Corporation Parcels Department; for H. Bridges (north Lancashire and Furness) and for Young's Express (Scotland).

(11) Bradford-Leicester Transport — Sheffield and Leeds (covering all West Riding) with transfer traffic for (a) United Automobile Services covering Durham, Northumberland and Cumberland (United also carried transfer traffic for south-east Scotland via Rogers of Earlston and for south-west Scotland via Caledonian Omnibus Co), (b) Reliance Carriers (Greatham), (c) Express Carriers (Bridlington), (d) Speed (Scarborough) (e) Coggill (North Riding) and (f) Clark's Boat (Scunthorpe).

(12) Donaldson Wright — Nottingham (serving Nottinghamshire and north Derbyshire) with transfer traffic for FTS for Skegness and coast.

(13) Giles and Bullen — King's Lynn and Norwich with transfer traffic for C. Watling (covering most of Norfolk and Suffolk).

(14) PX — Rushden, covering Northants, south Leicestershire, Bedfordshire, Huntingdonshire and Cambridgeshire.

(15) South Coast Carriers — Eastleigh and Yapton for West Sussex and East Hampshire.

(16) South Coast Carriers — Eastleigh and Bournemouth for west Hampshire, south Wiltshire and Dorset.

(17) Marshall, Son and Reading to their West Heath depot to connect with services covering Worcestershire, Herefordshire, north Gloucestershire and parts of Warwickshire.

(18) Venn and McPherson — Newport, Cardiff and Swansea, with services covering south and part of Central Wales.

(d) other carriers calling Mondays to Fridays and delivering en route.

(19) Derby Express Deliveries — Burton and south Derbyshire.

(20) W. Miles — Northampton via Rugby and Daventry — (also called at Coventry office).

(21) Wiggins — Hasely, for deliveries in rural Warwickshire.

(22) E. Phillips — Luton.

Coventry Depot

For trunks see Yardley depot; the Leicester trunk also acted as a collection and delivery vehicle. Coventry-based vans covered the area between those served by Yardley depot, Wiggins and Miles. Traffic was exchanged at Leicester with Blands serving the north-west of the county, Platts Bros serving the eastern part and Whiteman (Newark) for Lincolnshire. When there was surplus traffic out of Leicester the Birmingham service of Bamford Bros was used.

London (Malt Street) Depot

For trunks to and from Birmingham see Yardley depot. When northbound traffic exceeded southbound H. Brevitt of Willenhall was used for Black Country deliveries. Vans based on Malt Street served, roughly, the Metropolitan Police District, except the part covered by Chiswick depot.

Other carriers used from London

(1) Longton Transport for the Potteries.

(2) PX (base at Limehouse) for the East Midlands.

(3) J. Deamer and Son for Hitchin.

(4) E. R. Ives of Norwich for East Anglia.

(5) National Parcels (later Essex Carriers) of Thundersley for South Essex.

(6) Gamman and Dicker of Chatham (base at Silwood Street, Rotherhithe) for Kent.

(7) Routh and Stevens of East Hoathly for East Sussex.

(8) Astral Transport for West Surrey.

(9) C. Scott for Oxford.

(10) Carter, Paterson for West Sussex, Hampshire and Dorset.

(11) Pye and Counties (base at Southampton Street, Camberwell for Wiltshire and the West).

(12) All-British Carriers (base at Clapham Road) for South Wales.

(13) W. and J. Pargeter for High Wycombe.

London (Chiswick Common Road) Depot

For trunks to and from Birmingham, see Yardley depot. Chiswick-based vans served all West Middlesex and also Slough, Windsor, Kingston and Esher.

Gloucester (Merchants Road) Depot

Gloucester-based vans served the Stroud and Dursley industrial area; F. Walkley (Cinderford) provided a service to and from the Forest of Dean.

Bristol (Canning Street) Depot

For trunks to and from Birmingham, see Yardley depot. Because of heavy loads of bacon from Calne and Trowbridge, northbound traffic usually exceeded southbound; the surplus was trunked by Gibson, general haulier, with whom the depot was shared.

Bristol-based vans covered North Wiltshire and part of Somerset; they also delivered into and collected from the Bristol depots of:

(a) Pye and Counties for Devon (except Plymouth) and Cornwall (traffic for West Cornwall was passed on to Falmouth Transport)

(b) F. S. Huxham for Plymouth

(c) T. C. Binding for Clevedon

(d) Wild and White for parts of Somerset

They also connected with Guest, Wood and Ling for the Bath area and with Bath Tramways Motor Co for Central Wiltshire.

Appendix 3

Railway Charges for Merchandise Traffic*

SECTION (1)
The constitution and work of the Liaison Committee on Road Transport Rates

(1) The Liaison Committee consists of representatives of holders of 'A' and 'B' Licences of all the National Road Transport organisations, and was established in January 1938 following the issue of the Transport Advisory Council's Report on Service and Rates, and the announcement of the Minister of Transport that he intended in due course to introduce legislation on the lines suggested by the Council. The Liaison Committee was set up with the express purpose of evolving a road rate structure, together with the necessary adjuncts such as uniform terms and conditions of carriage.

(2) The Liaison Committee, which had hitherto been working along the lines of the report of the Transport Advisory Council, found itself confronted with a new situation in the shape of the Railways' claim for freedom from rate control. The Liaison Committee therefore felt that informal discussion might be helpful to both sides, and this suggestion was readily accepted by the Railways. In consequence a series of meetings had been held, and it has become possible to submit this memorandum as a joint memorandum to the Council.

SECTION (2)
Co-ordination a common objective

(3) Throughout the discussions both parties have kept in mind the view expressed by the Minister of Transport that due regard must be given to the ultimate objective of the co-ordination of all forms of transport. The Railways and the Liaison Committee are in agreement that this should be the objective, and they adhere to the view expressed by the Transport Advisory Council in its Report on Service and Rates that 'it is desirable to establish as great a degree of co-ordination as possible among the various forms of

*Joint Memorandum to the Transport Advisory Council by the Four Main Line Railway Companies and the Liaison Committee on Road Transport Rates

transport engaged in the carriage of goods, so as to ensure that each form of transport is used to the greatest national advantage'. Accordingly, nothing should be done to embarrass or postpone such objective.

(4) Both the Railways and the Liaison Committee are, however, convinced that it would not be practicable to apply to road transport the present railway rates structure with its elaborate classification, restrictions and obligations.

(5) Notwithstanding anything that follows herein, the Liaison Committee is of opinion that relief from restrictions should not be given to any form of transport, however necessary in other directions, if such relief should in any way prejudice the bringing about at an early date of rate structures applicable to all forms of public transport governed by suitable Tribunals.

(6) The Transport Advisory Council has already recommended that Road Hauliers should be afforded an opportunity to build up a rate structure for their own industry, and that co-ordination with other forms of transport should ultimately be effected through the medium of voluntary agreements. The Railways urge that the acceptance of their proposals, subject to the general safeguards proposed by them, will enable them to build up a new and simpler rate structure, and will also facilitate agreement between all forms of transport on such matters as a uniform system of rate control, correlated rate structures and standard conditions of carriage.

(7) The Liaison Committee, on the other hand, was not satisfied that the general safeguards proposed by the Railways were adequate, and as the outcome of the discussions which have taken place, certain special safeguards for the road haulage industry have been agreed to and accepted by both sides. On the basis of these safeguards, which are dealt with in detail later in this memorandum, the Liaison Committee raises no objection to the proposals of the Railways for the removal of statutory control of their merchandise charges, as contained in their memoranda to the Minister of Transport dates 23 November and

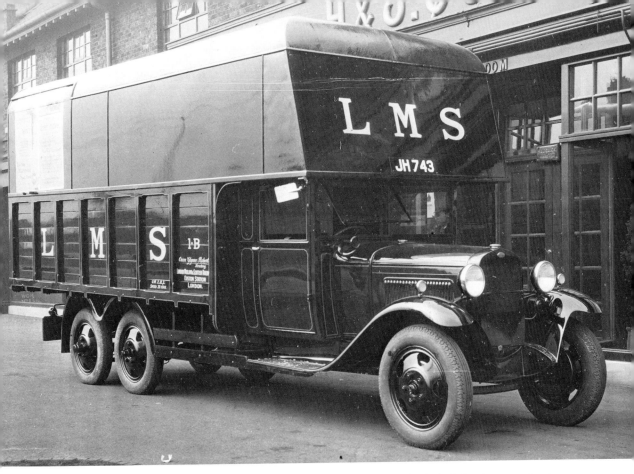

Above: *Ford produced a 6-wheel chassis to carry 6 ton in 1932; considering the solid structure of the body it is surprising that the unladen weight was as low as 2 ton 12 cwt 2 qr; unfortunately at that time the dividing line between 'motor car' and 'heavy motor car' was 2 ton 10 cwt, so this van was limited to 20 mph.*

8 December 1938, and in the statement entitled 'Amplification of the Railway Proposals' issued by the Transport Advisory Council on 13 January 1939.

SECTION (3)
Conditions of Carriage

(8) A considerable measure of agreement has already been reached among Road Hauliers in regard to standard conditions of carriage. Having regard to the views which have been placed before them, the Railways are prepared to withdraw their request for the repeal of the existing law relating to their own conditions of carriage, and are prepared to continue to accept the obligation to obtain the approval of the Rates Tribunal to any modifications which may subsequently be found desirable in order to secure uniformity of conditions of carriage for all forms of transport until such time as a comprehensive scheme embracing all forms of transport has been devised.

SECTION (4)
Objections to applications for 'A' and 'B' Licences

(9) The Liaison Committee has urged that, if the Railways are given the freedom in their charging powers for which they ask, it would no longer be appropriate for them to object to applications for the renewal of licences, and for the grant of additional licences to existing Road Hauliers, on the ground that adequate facilities by rail are available.

(10) The Railways point out that the right of objection under Section 11 of the Road & Rail Traffic Act, 1933, is conferred on *all* forms of transport, and in their view the exercise of this right has served as a means of placing before the Licensing Authorities information concerning existing transport facilities which is necessary for the proper discharge of their duties under the Act.

It is recognised that the Licensing Authorities in exercising their discretion either to grant or to refuse an application for an 'A' or 'B' Licence must, in the

125

terms of the Road & Rail Traffic Act, 1933, 'have regard primarily to the interests of the public generally, including those of persons requiring, as well as those of persons providing, facilities for transport'.

(11) The Railways hold the view that the principle thus embodied in the Act of 1933 is essential in any system of licensing if a properly co-ordinated system of transport is to be established but, with a view to affording Road Hauliers greater freedom in the meantime to negotiate within their industry voluntary agreements towards the establishment of such a system, the Railways are prepared to give an undertaking that, unless after consultation with the Central Consultative Committee (referred to in paragraph 14) either side feels that there are exceptional circumstances, they will not raise objection during the ensuing two years after they have been given their freedom whether the application is for:

(a) the renewal without any alteration, of existing 'A' or 'B' licences;
(b) the granting to existing hauliers of 'A' licences for additional vehicles;
(c) the granting to existing hauliers of additional 'B' licences for vehicles whose operations are limited to a radius not exceeding 25 miles

The Railways make it clear, however, that this undertaking is not to extend so as to preclude a railway company from giving, on request, information to a Licensing Authority concerning existing transport facilities which it provides, or from objecting to an application on the ground that the applicant has failed to comply with the conditions of the licence.

(12) The Liaison Committee acknowledges the value of this proposal but considers that the case law established up to the present by the objections of the Railways in the past would have the effect of visibly diminishing the value of the proposal. It is therefore accepted without prejudice to any subsequent action by either party in seeking amendment of the Road & Rail Traffic Act, 1933, in this respect.

(13) The Railways and the Liaison Committee agree that the industries shall co-operate as far as practicable with a view to securing due observance of the conditions attached to licences.

SECTION (5)
Proposed machinery designed to effect co-ordination

(14) With a view to facilitating co-operation between road and rail transport, both in regard to general measures of co-ordination and also in connection with matters more immediately affecting their own industries, it is agreed that a Central Consultative Committee of road and rail representatives shall be set up forthwith by voluntary arrangement between the parties. The Central Committee will draw up its own rules of procedure, and will have the right, as it thinks fit, to appoint Regional Committees. It is considered that machinery of this kind will afford valuable opportunities both for the free discussion of difficulties and also for considering constructive measures affecting the two forms of transport. As an immediate task it is agreed that the Central Consultative Committee will consider and formulate the principles on which voluntary agreements can be entered into in regard to the rates to be charged by road and rail for merchandise traffic, either generally or in respect of particular commodities or particular routes or areas, with due regard to the effect of such agreements on other interests.

(15) The Liaison Committee is convinced that, owing to the large number of operating units in the road haulage industry, adherence to voluntary agreements cannot be relied upon, and that some measure of statutory control is an essential preliminary to an attempt at co-ordination with other forms of transport. In order, therefore, to make joint agreements effective, it will be necessary to obtain statutory powers to secure their observance by all Road Hauliers between the points or in the areas affected. In the considered opinion of the Liaison Committee such powers are necessary, not at some future distant date when the country as a whole might be covered by a general comprehensive rate structure, but immediately agreements are entered into, not only on routes and in districts but even for specific traffic on those routes or in those distrcts. The Liaison Committee has therefore urged that any Bill repealing restrictions on railway charges should include clauses providing for machinery to sanction agreements and making the specified rates and conditions of carriage obligatory on all 'A' and 'B' licence holders and on the Railway Companies where concerned. The Liaison Committee submitted draft Clauses designed to achieve these objectives (see Appendix).

(16) The Railways have been deeply impressed by the importance attached to these proposals by the Liaison Committee. They recognise that the object of the draft clauses is to facilitate measures of co-ordination, and that in the absence of the proposed powers the Liaison Committee see no immediate prospect of being able to achieve co-ordination within their own industry. Having regard to the ultimate common objective, the Railways are prepared to agree to the principle of the

Right: *Karrier, of Huddersfield origin, was taken into the Rootes empire in 1934 and production was moved to Luton; this CK3 model of 1936 had the exceptional platform length of 17ft 4in.*

proposed Clauses for inclusion in any Bill removing railway restrictions.

SECTION (6)
Additional Special Safeguards for the Road Haulage Industry
(17) *Classification*

The Liaison Committee has felt some apprehension lest the removal of the present statutory requirements of the Railways in regard to classification should seriously retard, and possibly bring to a complete standstill, progress towards co-ordination. Their fear has been based on the ground that the Railways might attempt to function as freight carriers entirely without any classification of goods, and so produce innumerable complications and difficulties.

The Railways have, however, given an assurance that, while they are seeking to be free from the existing statutory requirements in regard to classification, they would of necessity have a voluntary system of classification in order to maintain their own commercial organisation on a sound footing. The removal of statutory control will, moreover, enable the Railways to modify their classification as may prove necessary in the interests of a co-ordinated system of rates.

(18) *Publication of Rates*

In this matter also the Railways have given an assurance that, though they seek to be free from the statutory obligation to publish rates, they will in practice publish lists of rates for the use of traders.

(19) *Undue Preference*

The Liaison Committee has felt some apprehension lest the freedom which the Railways seek from the present obligations in respect of undue preference might be used coercively to the detriment of the road haulage industry. The Railways point out that it is an explicit part of their proposals that they should charge *reasonable* rates, and that there should be a right of appeal by traders on the question of reasonableness to a tribunal, such as the Rates Tribunal referred to in the Appendix.

It is agreed that, in considering the question of reasonableness, the Tribunal should have regard to the rates charged for traffic of the same description carried under identical conditions between the same points, and also to the rates charged by competing forms of transport or agreed with them with a view to avoiding uneconomic transport rates.

(20) *Agreed Charges and Special Road Transport Contracts*

It is agreed by the Liaison Committee and the

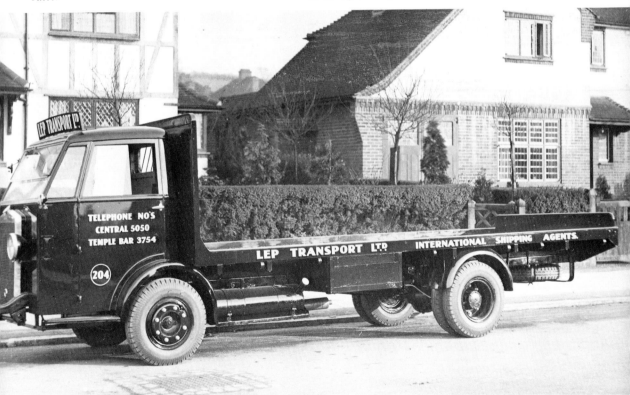

Railways that, as far as competitive traffic is concerned, the right of the Railways to make Agreed Charges, and the present practice of the Road Haulage industry to make Contract Charges other than on a per ton per mile basis, will have to come under review immediately any approach to the relationship of rail and road rates is attempted.

SECTION (7)
Conclusion
The Railways and the Liaison Committee urge that, in view of the agreement reached and the legislation proposed to give effect to it, the Government should defer any further legislation to give effect to the recommendations of the Transport Advisory Council on the setting up of a rate structure for a period of two years. If, after the lapse of two years, reasonable progress has not been made, it would be open to the Minister of Transport to introduce suitable legislation.

The proposals put forward in this memorandum involve only such legislation as is considered essential to give effect to measures of co-ordination agreed between the Rail and Road Haulage industries. Both parties desire to emphasise the importance which they attach to the scheme of voluntary consultation outlined in paragraph 14. It is their intention to set up this machinery of consultation forthwith and to co-operate fully in seeking a sound basis for the future development of their industries in the transport organisation of the country. They would point out that the statutory provisions which they here recommend contain ample safeguards for the protection of trade and industry in the form of a right of appeal to a judicial tribunal; whilst nothing in the proposals involves any interference with the right of the trader to use his own vehicles under a 'C' licence. The two forms of transport — Rail and Road — will continue to exist side by side as competitive but co-ordinated agencies. The competition will, however, be of a different kind, for, under a correlated system of rates, it will more than ever be the object, and the interest, of each to win traffic by the quality of the service which it renders.

ON BEHALF OF THE RAILWAY COMPANIES
(Signed) STAMP

ON BEHALF OF THE LIAISON COMMITTEE
(Signed) W. EDWARDS

6th February, 1939.

Appendix 4

Glossary*

'A' licence The licence granted to a public carrier (qv) under the Road and Rail Traffic Act, 1933. It was valid for five years and, theoretically, allowed complete freedom of operation. The licence specified the unladen weight of the vehicles authorised but did not authorise routes or lay down rates to be charged.

Abnormal load (Sometimes referred to as abnormal indivisible load.) A load which cannot be accommodated on any vehicle which conforms to the ordinary Construction and Use Regulations and which, therefore, has to be carried on a specially authorised type of vehicle.

Ancillary user A commercial vehicle owner whose business is not the provision of transport facilities for others, but who uses transport of his own to carry the goods he makes or deals in.

Appeal Tribunal The body set up under the Road and Rail Traffic Act, 1933, to consider appeals against the decisions of the Licensing Authorities. The Transport Act, 1947, transferred its functions to the Transport Tribunal, which has other duties in addition.

Applications and Decisions A publication issued regularly in each Traffic Area as a means of notifying interested parties of public sittings to be held by the Licensing Authority, of applications for new and varied licences and of the Authority's decisions in cases already dealt with.

Articulated vehicle (Sometimes contracted to articulator.) A composite vehicle composed of a tractor and trailer and arranged so that the trailer is partly superimposed on the tractor but can easily be detached therefrom. It is possible greatly to assist turn-round time by exchanging trailers at a terminal point instead of keeping the vehicle waiting while it is being unloaded and reloaded.

Attendant A person who rides on a vehicle to help in the loading or unloading and is not expected to drive.

'B' licence The licence granted to a limited carrier (qv) under the Road and Rail Traffic Act, 1933. It was

*Expressions used in road haulage during the period covered by this book. Most of these are still current, but some which were in common use in 1939 are now obsolete.

valid for two years and might (and almost always did) carry conditions specifying what type of goods might be carried 'for hire or reward' and within what radius. (See also A and C licence). The licensee was free carry his own goods without restriction.

Bank Same as deck (qv)

Bay May be either (a) a portion of a loading deck marked off for the temporary storage of goods for a particular area or (b) a rectangular recess in the deck face made so that vehicles may back in; sometimes used to facilitate side loading, sometimes to enable vehicles to stand without obstructing others.

Bin A term used in some districts for a portion of a loading deck, marked off for the temporary storage of goods for a particular destination; same as bay, in this sense. The term originated from the practice of early parcel carriers who collected very small packages which they sorted into actual bins or baskets for bulk delivery by rail.

Bolster An erection of two uprights and a crossbar (like goal posts) fitted to open lorries to enable long loads to be carried, projecting, if necessary above the cab.

Bonded Carman It is sometimes necessary to transfer from one warehouse to another imported goods on which duty has not been paid. This movement may only be made by vehicles registered with the Board of Customs and Excise, whose owners have entered into a bond making them liable should there be a loss of revenue through loss or damage. The specially registered vehicles carry a sign to this effect.

Bonneted Having the driver's cab behind the engine, which is, therefore, protected by a bonnet as on a private car; normal control means the same thing.

Boxvan A vehicle with fully enclosed body, the rear end being closed by doors, shutters or fixed tarpaulin sheets above a tailboard.

Buffer depot A place where stocks (usually of food stuffs) are held so that deliveries can be made locally in small lots and at short notice without recourse to the point of manufacture.

Bulk load carrier A carrier who usually only handles loads which enable a vehicle to go fully-loaded direct

from the picking-up point to the delivery point — in other words 'one pick-up, one drop.' Such carriers sometimes carry part-loads but usually avoid any consignments less than one ton in weight.

C and d work Collection and delivery work, done locally by vehicles acting as feeders to trunkers (qv); the c and d vehicles are normally smaller than the trunkers but this need not be so; some operators use vehicles which can work either on c and d or trunk.

Caller-off A man who assists in the checking of smalls by reading the labels of packages so that the checker can see if the goods received tally with the sender's consignment note.

Calibration Sand, gravel and similar materials are often sold by cubic measurement and it is compulsory for vehicles used on this work in England and Wales to be fitted with approved capacity indicators and also to be marked on the near side with the maximum cubic capacity and the tare weight.

Capacity indicator See Calibration.

Carriage forward An arrangement once common but now rarely used, where the consignee paid the carriage charges to the delivery carman.

'C' licence The licence which was granted to a private carrier (qv) under the Road and Rail Traffic Act, 1933 for the carriage solely of goods manufactured or processed by him or handled by him as a merchant. No charge for transport could be made in respect of goods carried on a C-licensed vehicle, unless the owner was a farmer and only then if he was carrying agricultural goods for a neighbouring farmer.

Checker A man employed to see that goods brought into a depot for transhipment agree with the entries on the sender's consignment note and that outgoing loads are accompanied by the proper documents.

Classification A term more usually associated in the past with goods traffic by rail, but one which in the period covered by this book was also heard in discussions on charges by road also, especially when there was talk of making rate agreements. Some smalls carriers who publish tariffs have a simple classification, dividing all the goods they normally carry into two or three categories and making different charges for the different classes. Goods may be classified either according to their bulkiness or their value or a combination of both (see also Rate and 'What the traffic will bear').

Claused signature An expression used when a recipient of goods adds after his signature, some remark indicating damage, pilferage or the like.

Clearing House An agency for putting persons who have goods to dispatch in touch with carriers who can provide the required facilities. It is unfortunate that the term has acquired a degree of opprobium in the industry because of the activities of unscrupulous individuals in the past, particularly in the 1920s. The well-organised and reputable clearing houses perform a useful function in saving a haulier from hunting for

Right: *Four examples of the AEC Mercury in the service of Watford Co-operative Society in 1935.*

work in towns where he has no office and they are of service to traders who can thus dispose of their traffic through one channel with a resultant simplification of accounting, etc. Clearing houses pass on to the hauliers who actually do the work the charges the traders agree to pay, less a commission, usually 10%.

Clear (or clean) signature A signature for the receipt of goods without any qualification. (See claused signature).

Collections clerk One who receives orders from customers for goods to be picked up and passes them on to an appropriate driver; a special employee for this work is usually only to be found on the staff of a large express carrying concern where a multiplicity of collections have to be arranged. With bulk load carriers the traffic manager usually allocates the work.

Company's risk Goods are carried at company's risk when the carrier accepts full liability for loss or damage in transit. Many operators have a modified form of liability (see Conditions of Carriage).

Conditions of carriage A haulier who is a good businessman will not accept goods for delivery without a clear understanding with his customer as to the extent of his liability in the event of loss, damage or delay. The degree of responsibility which he will or will not accept is set out in his conditions of carriage; these are usually printed on the consignment notes, on the back of letter-headings or in some other place where the customer can easily refer to them.

Co-operative group In some districts hauliers have banded themselves together, so that while they retain their identities they pool the available traffic and so save waste running; they form in effect a clearing house run by the group as distinct from the ordinary clearing hosue which usually owns no vehicles of its own.

Consequential loss Often a bone of contention between hauliers and customers; usually arises when a consignment arrives late and sales are lost as a result. This is one of the points which should be clarified in a haulier's conditions of carriage.

Consignment note The document made out by the sender of goods describing them and giving their weight and/or cubic measurement and handed by him to the carrier. Some carriers eventually return the customer's own note to him signed by the recipient; others make out their own documents and retain the original.

Construction and Use Regulations Regulations made by the Minister of Transport in the exercise of powers under the Road Traffic Act, 1930, whereby he controls the dimensions and weights of vehicles and their use on the roads in the interest of public safety.

Container A large box usually, but not necessarily, with a top and closed all round, into which goods can be stacked and then the whole load be lifted together on to a vehicle for transport; used for many years past in the furniture removal trade (where often termed lift-van) but now common for most commoditites.

Contract 'A' licence A form of A licence which was granted practically automatically to a public carrier in respect of a vehicle or vehicles which he could prove to the satisfaction of the Licensing Authority he was reserving exclusively for one particular hirer for a

minimum period of one year at a rate which would enable him to perform the work efficiently. The owner of the vehicle had to provide and pay the driver.

Contract hire Hiring a vehicle to a particular customer for his exclusive use for a definite period of time, either with or without a driver (see Contract A licence and Hiring margin). The contract may, and often does, provide for the vehicle to be designed and/or painted to the customer's requirements.

Cratch Tailboard.

Dead mileage Mileage run without a payload.

Deck A raised platform with its top surface usually about 3ft 6in from the ground level, from which vehicles can be more easily loaded and unloaded.

Delivery note It is the custom in some trades and with some carriers to leave with the consignee at the time of delivery a duplicate of the customer's consignment note.

Delivery sheet Smalls carriers usually enter all the deliveries for one particular driver on one or two long sheets, printed and ruled so that the consignee signs for the goods against the appropriate entry.

Diary The book in which a bulk load carrier enters orders received for transport; sometimes called a daybook.

Discrepancy advice Where goods have to be transhipped for final delivery it is sometimes found that what has been received does not tally with the details advised from the sending depot or customer; the discrepancy note advises the other party.

Dock Same as deck (qv)

Above: *An idea in 1927 to overcome a problem in the narrow streets of Manchester's warehouse quarters, where loading and unloading might be done at first-floor stages or through basement-chutes; a 2-ton Vulcan has been fitted with lifting gear by the Hydraulic Hoist Company and the van body has sliding side doors as well as a large tail-board with doors above at the rear.*

Right: *Before General Motors launched the Bedford, it offered the Chevrolet as a light lorry chassis, substituting on the 25cwt model (seen here) a 4-speed gearbox in place of the American 3-speed and fitting 4-wheel brakes and shock-absorbers; over two tons of oats were loaded on this truck and 4-wheel trailer.*

132

Documentation The paper work which has to be done to enable a carrier to have a permanent record of what he has carried and to be able both to charge his customer for his services and to prove that he has delivered the goods correctly.

Dolly A single-axle trailer with equipment which allows the fore-part of a load-carrying semi-trailer to be super-imposed on it, so that the vehicle so formed can itself be towed by a powered unit; the use of this device enables a semi-trailer to be used either as a portion of an articulated vehicle or in effect as a separate two-axle trailer drawn by a two or three axle prime mover.

Drawbar trailer A completely independent unit but without an engine and only capable of movement if attached by a bar (and usually by chains also) to some other vehicle which is powered (compare semi-trailer).

Dropside An open lorry with low side and tailboards, which can be swung down or lifted off for ease in loading or unloading.

Drug See pole-wagon.

Dump trucks or dumpers Heavily-built tipping vehicles specially constructed for working off roads on civil engineering sites, open-cast mines and quarries and similar rough places; reinforced steel bodies have a projection over the cab to protect drivers and engines from heavy falls of material.

Errand boy services Services using very small vehicles to give a quick delivery of shop parcels to private houses and similer facilities.

Exceptional rate A railway term to describe a charge which is less than the standard published tariff, the latter being calculated according to the classification of the goods and the mileage they are to be carried; obsolete since the passing of the Transport Act, 1953.

Express Carrier A carrier whose main business is the handling of smalls; the essential feature of his business is that his services are regular; he always goes irrespective of the volume of traffic to the districts he psrports to serve on the days he advertises his intention of doing so; usually he has a round of regular calls on customers whose traffic he collects for delivery to destinations either on his own vehicles or by transhipment to the properly-organised services of other express carriers.

Fifth-wheel The sloping plate with two hinged jaws which is fitted to the back of the tractor portion of an articulated vehicle as produced by some makers and which receives the nose of the trailer portion.

Fitting or fixture Term used in the Midlands to describe a portion of a deck marked off for traffic for a particular destination; same as bay or bin.

Flat A vehicle body without sides or tailboard and completely open.

Flat rate Some carriers, instead of charging each individual consignment from a particular customer according to its weight and destination, charge all traffic from that customer at the same rate per ton, or whatever other unit is agreed, irrespective of the size of consignments or where they are going to. This is a flat rate — often advantageous for tonnage but full of pitfalls when smalls are involved.

'F' licence This was not a licence in the sense of the A, B and C licences. Goods vehicles belonging to farmers were taxed at a preferential rate and it is the excise licence to which this term applied. Holders of F licences might, occasionally and in small quantities only, carry goods for other farmers but no charge might be made.

Forklift truck A device for moving goods which have been stacked on small platforms, called stillages or pallets; prongs on the truck are inserted under the pallets which can then be raised off the ground by mechanism built into the truck and the whole can be drawn away; many forklift trucks are built so that pallets and the goods on them can be stacked to a considerable height.

Forward control Originally meant the positioning of the driver of a commercial vehicle alongside or on top of the engine, so that he has not got the bonnet projecting in front of him; the term can be applied now to those chassis whichn have the engine under the floor or at the back.

Above: An expensive piece of advertising in 1928; the Ford van was repainted for the firm's 21st anniversary and was to revert to its original livery after a month; we don't know whether the flowers were real; a vanboy was carried as well as the driver and both wore uniforms.

Right: For most of the early 1920s, the most numerous light vans were undoubtedly those on T-model Ford chassis and it is amazing what Henry's baby stood up to; the owners of this van said that their flashing light display needed 109 bulbs and, apparently, the standard Ford dynamo and battery coped with this additional load, but one wonders if the lights went out when the vehicle stopped.

Functionat group The Road Haulage Association in addition to providing for the common interests of all hauliers caters for their special sectional interests through semi-autonomous functional groups. There are groups for agricultural hauliers, bulk liquid carriers, clearing houses, express carriers, heavy hauliers and machinery carriers, livestock carriers, long distance hauliers, meat carriers, milk carriers, sugar-beet hauliers, and tipping vehicle owners.

G.i.t Goods in transit; usually used in the phrase 'goods in transit insurance'.

G.o.h Goods on hand, ie goods which cannot be delivered. This may be because of an incorrect or defective address or the consignment may have been refused for some reason by the consignee. Should any of these things happen the carrier must immediately notify the sender or he may receive a claim for non-delivery.

Guidance sheet Same as Waybill (qv).

Heavy motor-car A mechanically propelled load- or passenger-carrier the unladen weight of which exceeds 3tons (originally $2\frac{1}{2}$tons); until May 1957 the maximum permitted speed for heavy motor-cars was only 20 miles per hour, compared zith 30 for lighter vehicles and this restriction had a considerable effect on vehicle design.

Hidden damage Damage which is only discovered when a consignment is unpacked. If the consignee has given a clear, unqualified signature, the carrier will usually not be legally liable, but it is the common practice at least to consider a claim if one is made within the time limit specified in the carrier's conditions of carriage. To protect their position some consignees add the words 'not examined' to their signature but is has been held that this is equivalent to a clear signature. This matter is a difficult one for all parties. Theoretically, the recipient should undo and examine all packages while the carrier waits but a moment's thought will show the impracticability of this.

Hiring margin Under the Road and Rail Traffic Act, 1933, a C-licensee had the right if he chose to ask for it, of hiring a specified number of vehicles without drivers. He had to supply the drivers. Because of this latitude, a C licence differed fundamentally from an A or a B, in which cases the licensee had to be in possession of certain specified vehicles. (Compare with Contract A licence, above.)

Above: *One of the problems of the 1920s was to produce buses with high seating capacity, having regard to the weight limits then in force, particularly axle-weights; the 6-wheeler seemed to be the answer but its use was not restricted to buses; many manufacturers adopted the idea for lorries and vans; one was Sydney Guy who started turning out 6-wheelers in 1925 and produced this van in 1927.*

Hopper Wagon A vehicle which discharges its load through an orifice in the floor.

Insurance The acceptance of liability to make good damage or loss to the thing insured. In haulage, the operator, in addition to insuring his vehicle like any other motor owner may, if he thinks fit, insure the loads he carries. The terms of his insurance and the premium demanded by the insurers will depend on the type of commodity to be handled, the degree to which the carrier wishes to accept liability and his record as an operator. Some hauliers arrange a complete cover, others only accept liability up to a certain amount per package, per ton or per load; in such cases they will usually arrange additional cover for their customer if required. Liability may be qualified by various clauses in the haulier's conditions of carriage. For certain types of goods he may refuse to accept liability altogether. Most goods in transit insurance policies are arranged through the usual insurance companies but it is not uncommon to employ brokers to arrange a Lloyd's policy.

Interworking This must not be confused with sub-contracting. Interworking exists when two or more carriers, each actually owning vehicles, agree to share certain traffic between them. It may be a certain class of traffic or all the traffic originating in a particular area, or the traffic moving over a certain route. In the latter case, the most common form of agreement is for one carrier to be at one end of the route and one at the other. In the case of full-load traffic the vehicles of either party are loaded as they happen to be available. If the agreement relates to smalls, it will certainly include the provision of trunk service. This is usually, but not necessarily, supplied by each party alternately, while each provides collection and delivery services at its own end. There have been interworking arrangements between smalls carriers extending over several hundred miles of road and involving more than two haulage companies. It is usual to agree standard charges for the terminal collection and delivery work and the provision of the trunk service, leaving the carrier who is in direct contact with a particular customer to get the best rate he can. Thus if two carriers, A and B, were running a service in 1939 between points C and D, they might have agreed that each terminal was worth 10s per ton and the trunk 20s per ton, making 40s in all. If A could have obtained 45s for a particular traffic he would have been 5s a ton better off; if however, he could only have obtained 35s he would have been 5s down, because he would still have to pay B 10s for delivery, plus 20s on those occasions when B worked the trunk. Nevertheless, there might have been circumstances in which A agreed to carry at the lower rate. Of course with bulk loads, the question of splitting between trunk and terminal charges does not arise. Usually with smalls, terminals are not expressed in a flat rate per ton but are broken down into a scale, having cadences according to weight.

Jack-truck The same in principle as a fork-lift truck, but worked manually by an operator walking instead of by a self-propelled machine; a finger-shaped device is passed under a flat truck or small platform, on which goods have been stacked, the platform is raised slightly off the ground and so can be drawn away.

Lead The single-journey mileage between a point of collection and a point of delivery.

Legal break The colloquial way of referring to the rest of at least half an hour which every goods vehicle driver had to take after five and a half hours' continuous driving or work in connection with his load. (At the time of writing the law regarding this break is likely to be altered to conform to EEC regulations.)

Licensed carman Members of the Worshipful Company of Carmen have the right to stand for hire at certain points in the City of London providing their vehicles are branded every August and carry a brass registration number, issued for a small fee by the Keeper of Guildhall.

Licensing Authority Great Britain is divided into eleven Traffic Areas and in each a Licensing Authority for Goods Vehicles is responsible for deciding whether operators' licences under the Transport Act, 1968, shall be granted. During the period covered by this book, the relevant statute was the Road and Rail Traffic Act, 1933. In every area (except the Metropolitan) the Licensing Authority is also the Chairman of the Traffic Commissioners who control passenger vehicle licensing. In the Metropolitan Area the Licensing Authority is also the Traffic Commissioner but sits alone in the latter capacity without representatives of the local authorities such as sit with the other chairmen. Because of this duality of function the Licensing Authorities are colloquially referred to as the Traffic Commissioners even when haulage is being discussed.

Lift-van A closed wooden or metal box which can be lifted on or off a vehicle when loaded. Lift-vans have been in use for a century or more for household removals originally by transhipment between horse-drawn trolley and railway flat wagon. (See Container.)

Limited carrier One who had a B licence under the Road and Rail Traffic Act, 1933. A limited carrier was one who could either carry his own goods or could carry other people's goods for hire or reward. When he carried his own goods he was as unrestricted as a private or C carrier, but when he acted as a public carrier he might be limited as to the traffic he might carry and the radius in which he might carry it.

Locomotive In road transport law, a mechanically propelled vehicle not constructed to carry a load, the unladen weight of which exceeds $7\frac{1}{4}$tons; locomotives weighing not more than $11\frac{1}{2}$ton are called light locomotives and those which do exceed this figure heavy locomotives.

Log sheet The colloquial name for the record of hours of work and loads carried which had to be kept accurately be all holders of licences issued under the Road and Rail Traffic Act, 1933.

Low-loader A vehicle (usually a trailer or semi-trailer) the floor of which is closer to the ground than the usual 3-4 feet; the whole floor of the low loader may be at a uniform low level or it may be constructed so that most of the floor forms a well between the two axles; in the latter case normal diameter wheels may be used; otherwise special small wheels are usually employed although there are models in which a narrow platform is slung between ordinary sized wheels.

Luton van In the 1920s to deal with the bulky straw hats which were the staple trade of Luton (Beds) vans working from that town were built with an extension over the driver's cab in order to give the maximum space. This was a new idea and such vehicles were immediately dubbed Luton vans. Before long the space over the cab came to called colloquially the Luton.

Manchester load A colloquial term in the Midlands describing a van loaded in such a way that it appears full when viewed at the back, but in fact has very little inside at the front; origin uncertain.

Mate One who travels on a vehicle to help load and unload but does not drive.

Mechanical horse A three-wheeled tractor originally designed to replace the horses employed by the railway companies in goods yards, dock areas and inner town deliveries: its main characteristic is its extreme manoeuvrability and small turning-circle.

Motor car In road transport law, a vehicle constructed to carry loads or passengers and not exceeding 3ton unladen (see heavy motor-car).

NAFWR National Association of Furniture Warehousemen and Removers, Ltd.

Normal control A vehicle with the driver sitting behind the engine.

Normal user Under the Road and Rail Traffic Act, 1933, an applicant for an A or B licence had to tell the Licensing Authority on the application form 'the facilities for the transport of goods intended to be provided by him under the licence for other persons including particulars of the district within which, or the places between which, it was intended that the authorised vehicles would normally be used for the purpose of carrying goods for hire or reward'.

Objector When an application for a new A or B licence or a variation of an existing one was published in *Applications and Decisions* objection to the proposal might 'be made by persons who are already providing facilities, whether by means of road transport or any other kind of transport, for the carriage of goods for hire or reward in the district, or between the places which the applicant intends to serve'. Under the Road and Rail Traffic Act, 1933, the onus was on the applicant, in effect, to prove the unsuitability of existing facilities in relation to his proposals.

OR Owner's risk — generally implying that while the carrier will take responsibility for delivery, he will not, because of the nature of the goods, accept any liability for damage or pilferage.

Overtopping Loading goods on an upper deck of a lorry, so constructed that the upper deck is easily removable.

Paid on (or paid out) When goods consigned carriage forward have to be transhipped the first carrier may not know what charges will be made by the second; he therefore declares what he wants (this is the paid-on or paid-out), leaving the final carrier to add his own charges.

Pallet A structure on which or into which a number of articles can be assembled so that the whole lot can be moved in any direction at one movement; the simplest and original form is the small flat platform called a stillage constructed so that a fork can be inserted under it for lifting and moving. From this have developed a variety of forms to suit particular trades, notably cage pallets which, having sides, can be used for packages which do not stack in a homogeneous manner.

Parcels A vague term but roughly, packages up to about 21-28lb ie smaller than smalls (qv).

Part-load Anything less than the full capacity of the vehicle.

Payload The difference between the empty and the laden weight of a vehicle.

Pick-up A vehicle about the size of a large private car but with the body adapted so that goods can easily be carried.

Platform Can either mean the same as deck or can refer to the part on which goods are loaded on an open vehicle.

Platform lorry A vehicle with a completely open, flat and unsided body.

Pole wagon A vehicle without a body, but consisting of two axles connected by a long wooden or metal pole and with bearers constructed above the axles and parallel to them so that trees, long pipes and similar articles can be carried easily and lifted on and off by crane; the wagon may be simply a trailer or it may be part of an articulated unit; some are fitted with

Left: *How Harris Road Services of Lostock Gralam used a dolly to convert a semi-trailer so that it could be towed behind a 4-wheeler.*

Above: *An interesting miscellany of handling aids at a dockside wharf; the Leyland Beaver, as an articulator, could also draw a 4-wheel trailer within dock limits.*

telescopic poles so that the length of the articles to be carried can be varied.

Prime mover The tractor portion of an articulated outfit.

Prime rate The rate charged by a clearing house to its customer.

Private carrier An operator who carries nothing but the goods he makes or handles in the course of his business as a trader; one who does not carry 'for hire or reward'; under the 1933 Act, a C licensee.

Public carrier One who carries solely 'for hire or reward'; under the 1933 Act, an A licensee.

Public enquiry Unless a variation were trivial, a Licensing Authority would hear an application for the variation of an A or B licence in public and would always do so for a new or renewed licence. The same procedure applies now with the operators' licences, which have replaced the carriers' licences introduced by the 1933 Act.

Queen Mary A low-slung trailer of light construction with lattice-work sides originally designed for carrying aeroplane wings; with its tractor, the articulated vehicle so formed was normally about 60ft long.

Queries clerk The person who deals with complaints of delay, loss and damage in the office of a smalls operator.

Rail Janker A heavy platform vehicle fitted with a turn-table at the rear-end and linked by steel rails with a trailer, so that long and heavy girders, etc, can be carried.

Rate The charge made for carriage or hire expressed as so much a ton or so much an hour.

Rave A substantial piece of beading fixed along the edge of the platform on an open lorry — not high enough to form a side but sufficiently high to prevent loads sliding off sideways.

RE Returned empty.

Rigid Refers to vehicles having more than two axles and not articulated.

Road Haulage Wages Board The Board, set up by the Road Haulage Wages Act, 1938, consisted of equal numbers of employers' and employees' representatives, plus three independent members; its awards, after confirmation by the Minister of Labour were binding on A and B licensees as minimum payments and conditions.

Roll-up tank A receptacle for carrying liquids, which, being made of a flexible material, instead of metal, collapses when emptied and can then be folded up into a relatively small space.

Road & Rail Central Conference As a result of negotiations between the four main-line railways and representatives of the haulage industry in 1939 it was agreed that both sides should work towards a common classification of merchandise traffic and a common rate structure. The Road and Rail Central Conference and subsidiary Conferences in each Traffic Area were set up to do this. A great deal of time was spent in studying the problem, but after the war there was a complete reversal of policy by the railways. In 1953 they secured freedom to jettison the old conceptions of classification and standard charges. The Conference, therefore, faded out.

Semi-trailer A trailer which cannot be towed without being super-imposed on a tractor to form an articulated unit.

Scale Many hauliers, especially those handling parcels, smalls and part-lots, do not quote a uniform rate irrespective of the quantity of a particular commodity they may carry, but charge on a graded scale, the effect of which is that the smaller the consignment the higher is the rate per ton. This is to compensate for the additional work involved in dealing with small lots.

Section 19 The colloquial way of referring to the legal restrictions on drivers' hours, which were based on section 19 of the Road Traffic Act, 1930.

Sheet Usually means the large tarpaulin which is spread over the load on an open vehicle but may also mean a delivery sheet (qv).

Shunter The man who drives a trunk vehicle at the collection or delivery end and not on the trunk portion of the journey.

Sided An open vehicle with sides (usually not very high) but no roof to the body.

Skids Two pieces of stout wood or metal of equal length, connected by metal cross pieces like the rungs of a ladder, and having hooks at one end which enable the skids to be attached to a wagon or loading bank; barrels and heavy cases can then be slid down them.

Smalls Roughly speaking, consignments of less than a ton and larger than parcel post will take; the railways now regard consignments of less than two tons as smalls.

Special type A vehicle which does not conform with the Construction and Use Regulations (usually because it is too wide or too long) and can, therefore,

Left: *Spillers ordered this unusual trailer from Dyson of Liverpool.*

only be operated under special conditions as laid down in Motor Vehicles (Authorisation of Special Types) General Order, 1957.

Split delivery Strictly speaking means that a bulk load of identical or similar goods is conveyed as one consignment from the point of origin to some distant place and there broken down into small lots for ultimate delivery; this method, therefore, contrasts with that in which the sender himself makes up all the individual consignments, even although they all go together on the same vehicle to the same destination town. In practice, the railways have for many years been willing to treat all smalls sent to the same town at the same time as one consignment for charging (plus a split delivery charge), so saving the sender money, and their example has been followed by some carriers.

Square Deal The proclaimed object of the railway companies in 1938 when they launched a campaign to secure a relaxation of some of their statutory obligations (see Road & Rail Central Conference).

Station wagon See Pick-up.

Statutory attendant The Road Traffic Act, 1930, made it compulsory for vehicles drawing a trailer to carry an attendant as well as the driver, the reason being that at that time the brakes on most trailers were worked from the towing vehicle manually.

Stillage See Pallet.

Sub-contractor One who carries traffic on behalf of another carrier or of a clearing house and has no direct contact with the sender of the goods; the term is not, however, applied to the parties in an inter-working arrangement, since in effect, a pool has been established in such cases and both parties have equal status.

Tanker (or tank-wagon) A vehicle carrying a tank in which can be conveyed liquids or powders in bulk.

Terminal May mean either (a) a building in which collections and deliveries are sorted, incoming vehicles unloaded and outgoing ones loaded or (b) the charge made for collection or delivery. In railway parlance there is a slight difference — terminal means such work as sheeting and unsheeting wagons and not collecting or delivering.

Tilt A hood of canvas or other material stretched over hooped sticks to close in an otherwise open vehicle, hence colloquially applied to any vehicle so fitted.

Tipper A vehicle fitted with a ram which can lift the body upwards or sideways at an angle sufficiently great for the load to shoot out by gravity.

Tonnage Greater than smalls.

Tractor A mechanically propelled unit not designed to carry a load itself but capable of pulling a loaded vehicle or of having a semi-trailer superimposed upon it to form an articulated vehicle. In law, any tractor weighing more than $7\frac{1}{2}$ton is a locomotive.

Traffic Area England and Wales are divided into 10 Traffic Areas and Scotland is another Area. Each Traffic Area is the territory in which a particular Licensing Authority is responsible for administering the control of the haulage industry according to the various Acts governing it.

Traffic Commissioner See Licensing Authority.

Traffic Court Colloquial term for a public hearing by a Licensing Authority of applications for the grant or variation of operators' (formerly of carriers') licences.

Traffic Manager The official of a transport company who is responsible for securing business and seeing that the traffic is efficiently handled.

Traffic Pool See Inter-working and Co-operative Group

Trailer A load-carrying vehicle without any means of self-propulsion and intended for towing by a steam or motor vehicle.

Trailer plate At the period with which this book deals a trailer when being towed on the road had to carry at the back in a conspicuous place a sign with the letter T on a square plate.

Tramp A vehicle which is not employed on any regular run but goes to any destination for which its owner can get a load.

Transhipment Changing over goods from one vehicle to another; may be done to secure better loading, but in smalls operations is an essential procedure as, in general, different vehicles are used for collection and delivery from those employed in trunking.

Truck This term is used either in the same sense as lorry or as indicating a manually-operated device (normally 2-wheeled) for moving sacks and other items too heavy to be manhandled along a loading-deck or from a vehicle to customers' premises and vice versa; sometimes referred to as a barrow although the latter is, strictly speaking, something expressly designed for hand propulsion in the streets.

Trunking Running from one terminal point to another, usually without delivering or collecting en route.

Trunker A vehicle used for trunking.

Turn round The time taken to unload, reload and dispatch a vehicle on a fresh journey when it reaches a terminal point.

Utility See Pick-up.

Van A covered vehicle in contrast to a lorry; it may be completely enclosed as a boxvan or open at the rear as a tilt.

Vehicle Report Book Most operators have a book in a convenient place where incoming drivers can report vehicle defects in writing. Sometimes these are printed sheets listing all the principal components of a vehicle so that a driver has no excuse for forgetting to report anything wrong.

Waybill A survivor of coaching days, when the waybill for each vehicle detailed the names of the passengers and details of goods carried and destinations; still used for the list of mixed items sent by a trunker on an express carrier's inter-urban service and, sometimes, also for the local delivery sheet.

'What the traffic will bear' A century-old method of describing the principle which governed railway charging from the beginning until 1953, ie to charge mainly according to the value of the goods carried and with little regard to their bulk — thus a ton of gold was charged at a considerably higher rate than a ton of chickens' feathers. Road hauliers have usually charged on the basis of weight in relation to the space occupied and with little regard to intrinsic value. The growth of road transport undermined the railway finances, since they were based on the idea of making the more valuable commodities pay for the cheaper carriage charges levied on raw materials and the like.

Zonal charge Instead of quoting a separate rate from a particular centre to every place within a certain county of clearly defined region, carriers will often, for the mutual convenience of themselves and their customers, quote a zonal rate, ie will charge the same to each place in the zone.

Index

143